The Power of ONE

Gail L. Thompson

The Power of ONE

How You Can Help or Harm African American Students

CORWIN
A SAGE Company

For information:

Corwin
A SAGE Company
2455 Teller Road
Thousand Oaks, California 91320
(800) 233-9936
Fax: (800) 417-2466
www.corwinpress.com

SAGE Ltd.
1 Oliver's Yard
55 City Road
London EC1Y 1SP
United Kingdom

SAGE India Pvt. Ltd.
B 1/I 1 Mohan Cooperative
   Industrial Area
Mathura Road, New Delhi 110 044
India

SAGE Asia-Pacific Pte. Ltd.
33 Pekin Street #02-01
Far East Square
Singapore 048763

Printed in the United States of America.

Library of Congress Cataloging-in-Publication Data

Thompson, Gail L., 1957–
The power of one: how you can help or harm African American students / Gail L. Thompson.
      p. cm.
Includes bibliographical references and index.
ISBN 978-1-4129-7676-3 (pbk.)
   1. African American students—Psychology. 2. African American students—Services for. 3. Teacher-student relationships. 4. Motivation in education. 5. Racism in education. I. Title.

LC2717.T49 2010
371.829'96073—dc22   2009032761

This book is printed on acid-free paper.

09   10   11   12   13   10   9   8   7   6   5   4   3   2   1

Acquisitions Editor:	Dan Alpert
Editorial Assistant:	Megan Bedell
Production Editor:	Libby Larson
Copy Editor:	Jenifer Dill
Typesetter:	C&M Digitals (P) Ltd.
Proofreader:	Sally Jaskold
Indexer:	Gloria Tierney
Cover and Graphic Designer:	Rose Storey

Contents

Acknowledgments

As always, I am grateful to God; my husband, Rufus; my children, Nafissa, NaChe', and Stephen; my son-in-law, Derrick; sister, Tracy Harkless; and other family members—for their ongoing support and encouragement. I would also like to thank Dan Alpert, a wonderful, enthusiastic, and supportive editor, and Allyson Sharp and Megan Bedell for their hard work and encouragement. My mentor, Dr. David E. Drew, former colleague, Dr. Lourdes Arguelles, friends Cynthia Hebron, Mary David, Deborah Tavasti, Sharon Holmes-Johnson, Dr. Angela Louque, Malinda West, Ardelia Rhone, and colleagues Dr. Delacy Ganley, Dr. Anita Quintanar, Lisa Loop, and Dr. Barbara DeHart have also been extremely supportive. I am also grateful to my pastor, Dr. Terrence Rhone, and his wife, Elizabeth, for constantly reminding African American youth and adults that a good education is invaluable.

About the Author

 **Dr. Gail L. Thompson,** a professor of Education at Claremont Graduate University, has written five books: *A Brighter Day: How Parents Can Help African American Youth; Up Where We Belong: Helping African American and Latino Students Rise in School and in Life; African American Teens Discuss Their Schooling Experiences; What African American Parents Want Educators to Know;* and *Through Ebony Eyes: What Teachers Need to Know But Are Afraid to Ask About African American Students,* a book that has received a considerable amount of attention from educators, talk show hosts, and news reporters across the nation. One of her essays was published in *USA Today,* and her work has been published in numerous academic journals and three edited books.

Dr. Thompson has appeared on PBS television's *Tony Brown's Journal,* National Public Radio, and Tavis Smiley's radio show. She has been interviewed for *Scholastic Instructor* and *Inside Higher Education* and has been quoted in numerous newspaper articles. She has served as a reviewer for the Educational Broadcasting Network, Millmark Education, Houghton Mifflin, and several academic journals, and has done presentations, keynote addresses, workshops, and consultant work throughout the United States and two presentations in Canada. Dr. Thompson, who taught junior high and high school for 14 years, is a member of the California Department of Education's African American Advisory Committee. She has received several awards from student organizations and a civic award for teaching. In 2009, Claremont Graduate University gave her its Distinguished Alumna award.

Dr. Thompson is married to Rufus Thompson, a veteran educator, with whom she has three children: Dr. Nafissa Thompson-Spires; NaChe', a college undergraduate; and Stephen, a college undergraduate.

Introduction

Why Alarm Bells Should Be Ringing in Our Heads

In July 2008, I received three e-mails and a telephone call that were similar to many others I've gotten during the last 11 years. The telephone call was from a school administrator in California. The e-mails were from district-level school administrators in Virginia, Florida, and California. They all wanted the same thing—help in doing a better job of educating African American K–12 students. Like countless educators throughout the nation, these administrators realized that in spite of the abundance of research on the achievement gaps, many teachers—perhaps even most—*still* need help in this area. Unfortunately, most teacher-preparation programs are *still* failing to adequately prepare teachers to work effectively with African American students and other students who have historically been shortchanged by the education system, and most professional development for teachers either doesn't last long enough to do an adequate job or fails to address this issue at all. This is disturbing because, in spite of the No Child Left Behind Act, recent statistics suggest that the public school system in the United States is failing an alarming number of African American, American Indian, Alaska Native, and Latino K–12 students.

- High school **dropout rates** have *decreased* for all racial and ethnic groups during the past 30 years. However, black and Hispanic students continue to have much higher dropout rates than whites. In 2006, 5.8% of whites, 10.7% of blacks, and 22.1% of Hispanics dropped out.[1]
- High school **graduation rates** for the "Principal School Districts Serving the Nation's 50 Largest Cities" range from 24.9% to 77.1%.[2]
- Suburban school districts tend to have much higher graduation rates than urban districts.[3]

1

- In terms of **race/ethnicity,** the national average graduation rates were 76.2% for whites; 53.4% for blacks; 57.8% for Hispanics; 80.2% for Asian/Pacific Islanders; and 49.3% for American Indian/Alaska Natives.[4]
- In terms of **gender**, Asian/Pacific Islanders had the *highest* graduation rate for males (76.5%), and black males (46.2%) and American Indian/Alaska Native males (44.6%) had the lowest. Among females, Asian/Pacific Islanders had the highest graduation rate (82.1%), and American Indian/Alaska Natives (50%) and black females (59.6%) had the lowest.[5]

These statistics should alarm any concerned American, but especially educators, because the level of education a person attains largely determines the type of future that individual will have. Many of the social problems that plague our nation are linked to poverty, and of course, a good education is the only legitimate way that most low-income children will be able to escape from poverty. In fact, according to the U.S. Census Bureau, individuals who don't complete high school are twice as likely as those who do to end up living in poverty as adults, and those who don't complete high school are nearly six times more likely than individuals who earn a bachelor's degree to end up living in poverty as adults.[6] More than 12 million U.S. children under the age of 18 live in poverty, and African American and Latino children are a lot more likely than white children to be living at or below the poverty level.[7]

Poverty is also linked to crime rates. During the past few years, on average, more than 2 million juvenile arrests have occurred each year in the United States.[8] Furthermore, the U.S. Department of Justice reported the following:

- "If recent incarceration rates remain unchanged, an estimated 1 out of every 15 persons (6.6%) will serve time in a prison during their lifetime."[9]
- "Lifetime chances of a person going to prison are higher for men (11.3%) than for women (1.8%) [and higher for] blacks (18.6%) and Hispanics (10%) than for whites (3.4%)."[10]
- "Based on current rates of first incarceration, an estimated 32% of black males will enter State or Federal prison during their lifetime, compared to 17% of Hispanic males and 5.9% of white males."[11]

According to the Children's Defense Fund, race and poverty are the two factors that most likely determine who will end up in prison, and black and Latino youth are a lot more likely to be arrested and incarcerated than white youth.[12] Unfortunately, because of various policies that have been implemented, the public school system now plays a vital role in "funneling" many black and Latino youth into the "school-to-prison pipeline."[13] In other words, instead of equipping these youth from low-income backgrounds with an education that will enable them to escape from poverty, the public school system contributes to ensuring that many will not only remain in poverty, but that some youth will never have a chance to improve the quality of their lives. As the NAACP Legal Defense and Educational Fund concluded:

> Criminal justice policy in the United States has for some time now spurned rehabilitation in favor of long and often permanent terms of incarceration, manifesting an overarching belief that there is no need to address root causes of crime and that many people who have committed crimes can never be anything but "criminals." These policies have served to isolate and remove a massive number of people, a disproportionately large percentage of whom are people of color, from their communities and from participation in civil society.[14]

As a veteran educator with teaching experience in both underperforming schools and in universities, and as a researcher and education consultant who has listened not only to the concerns of educators but also to those expressed by African American students and African American parents, writing this book became my way of addressing an ongoing problem that I have devoted the last 11 years to tackling: How can educators do a better job of educating African American children?

If you're a K–12 teacher, counselor, principal, or vice principal, this book can empower you. One of its main features is that you can use it in the privacy of your own home. However, if you are a teacher educator, you can use this book as a required or recommended text for prospective and current teachers. If you are an education consultant, mentor-teacher, or district-level administrator, this book will enable you to deal with any issues that *you* need to face about African American K–12 students and their parents. It will also allow you to provide quality in-depth professional-development training to small or large groups of educators *after* you have read the book, completed the exercises, and worked on your own personal roadblocks. Then, you can use the book to train new and veteran teachers. Here's a summary of the benefits:

ELEVEN WAYS THAT THIS BOOK CAN BENEFIT READERS

The book will help you do the following:

- Increase your efficacy with African American K–12 students
- Uncover mental baggage that may impede your progress
- Examine your views about racism and race relations
- Identify the *personal* benefits of becoming a more effective educator of African American students
- Deal with obstacles to effective classroom management

- Learn how to improve your relations with African American parents
- Tackle actual classroom scenarios and become aware of problems that some educators have had with African American students
- Learn the answers to questions that many educators have about African American students
- Compare your views to those of other educators
- Become a wiser, more effective, and more courageous educator
- Become committed to engaging in lifelong professional development

Besides the fact that you can use it for personal and professional development at home as well as in formal settings, this book is unique for several other reasons. First, it contains stories from teachers, parents, former students, and other individuals about their experiences. Second, it contains actual classroom scenarios. Third, each chapter contains exercises that I designed to help you (a) examine your personal beliefs about important issues and (b) become a better educator as a result of what you learn about yourself and these issues. I designed most of the exercises for you to complete on your own, but each chapter also includes a group exercise that you can complete with other educators. Fourth, throughout the book, I have included feedback from over 600 educators and individuals connected to schools in three distinctly different states—California, Texas, and Minnesota—which will permit you to compare your views and experiences with those of the respondents. Fifth, I have devoted an entire chapter to advice from teachers about how educators can prepare students for standardized tests. Sixth, Chapter 8 contains numerous questions from educators and other individuals for you to not only *read*, but also to attempt to answer based on the information that you learned from previous chapters.

MOVING FORWARD

INTRODUCTORY EXERCISE: AN ATTITUDE CHECK

(Note: You might need additional space for this exercise and others throughout the book. Therefore, you may prefer to record all of your answers in a journal that you can update and refer to on an ongoing basis.)

Before you read the next chapter, please answer the following questions:

1. How do you feel about reading a book that focuses on African American students?

_____

_____

2. Are you willing to engage in self-reflection as you read this book?

    _____

    _____

3. Are you willing to at least *attempt* to complete every single exercise to the best of your ability?

    _____

    _____

4. Will you try your best to answer every question and complete every exercise as *honestly* as you can?

    _____

    _____

5. Now, review your answers to the first four questions, and explain what your answers reveal about you.

    _____

    _____

6. Did any issue(s) surface that could prevent you from benefiting from reading this book?

    _____

    _____

    If so, what do you need to do *before* you read the rest of the book?

    _____

    _____

Of course, I can't peer over your shoulder and read your answers. But I do know that if you sincerely want to increase your efficacy with African American students, you can. In other words, if you *choose* to, you can become a better educator of African American students. The choice is yours. If you want to learn some of the ways to do so, and if you are courageous and willing to engage in honest self-reflection, then get ready to turn the page. If you have chosen to accept this challenge, let me be the first to commend you for deciding to embark upon one of the most mind-changing and revolutionary journeys that you will take during your career as an educator.

PART I

Beliefs, Mindsets, and Baggage

1

Identifying the **Personal** *Benefits of Increasing Your Efficacy With African American Students*

One day, during the period when I was writing this book, I met an African American security guard at a local elementary school. As I passed by a school while finishing the last mile of my morning walk, she said, "Hello." For some reason, that simple hello led to an extensive conversation. At first, we discussed weight loss and exercise. I learned that she'd recently lost a lot of weight and would soon be celebrating her 50th birthday. We also spoke about other things and realized that we had more in common than an interest in fitness. In fact, it turned out that we had several mutual acquaintances. When the conversation turned to the topic of education, she began to speak about her own K–12 school experiences. The story that she shared illustrates the enormous amount of power that teachers wield over students and how both good and bad teachers can have long-term effects on them. I asked her if I could borrow the notepad and ink pen that were protruding from the pocket of her uniform shirt so that I could take notes in order to share her story with you. In the next section, you'll read Nyala's story (throughout this book, I have changed the names of the individuals whom I describe), and then, I'll ask you to complete a related exercise.

NYALA'S STORY: "I GAVE UP BECAUSE EVERYBODY HAD GIVEN UP ON ME."

Nyala grew up in Alabama, in a large family that included her parents and her 13 siblings. At first, she and her siblings attended all-black schools. Although the U.S. Supreme Court had outlawed segregation in public schools four years before her birth, at the time when she started elementary school, segregation was still common where she lived. But things were about to change. Ten years after the Supreme Court's ruling, local government officials finally decided to comply. Therefore, when Nyala entered third grade, it was at an "integrated" school instead of at the all-black school where she had spent the previous three years. At the new school, she learned two powerful lessons. These lessons were not part of the formal curriculum that her teacher taught, but rather from the "hidden curriculum."

The first lesson that she learned was that in spite of their dark skin, she and her six African American classmates were invisible. Nyala learned this after repeatedly raising her hand, only to find that her teacher never saw it—or at least pretended not to. No matter how long Nyala held her hand in the air, her teacher never called on her.

The second lesson she learned was that she had been subjected to inequality of educational opportunity. It turned out that at the all-black school, the books were old, outdated, and less challenging than the ones at her new school. "We actually didn't have the material to keep up," Nyala explained. "I was a better reader than most of the kids at the black school," she said. However, at the predominantly white school, she realized that she and her African American classmates had weaker reading skills than their white peers. According to Nyala, "In the black school, the books didn't prepare us for the books they were reading in the white school, [but] in the white school, they never let us [the African American students] read [orally] in class."

Before long, Nyala was feeling horrible about both herself and school. Because of her weak reading skills, she said, "I felt like a jackass! That school didn't fertilize my mind or my spirit. The teacher didn't care about me. I gave up because everybody had given up on me."

Whereas having poor reading skills and being ignored by her teacher caused Nyala to become apathetic about school, a more pressing and more embarrassing issue also contributed to her hatred of the predominantly white school. Because the teacher refused to call on her when she raised her hand, Nyala often urinated on herself. Being ignored meant that the teacher never knew when her hand was raised to *answer* a question, or when it was raised to *ask* an important question: for permission to go to the restroom. "When I put my hand up and my head down, that meant that I had wet on myself," she remarked. "I wasn't the only one." Evidently, her African American classmates were also forced to wet their pants periodically, and her siblings in other classes at that elementary school met the same fate. "My mother had 14 kids," Nyala explained, "and six of us were in elementary school. My brothers and sisters were having the same problem. I had to learn to control my bladder." The situation reached a terrible climax on the day when one of her brothers, a fifth grader, actually had a bowel movement on himself in class. "That's when my mother went to the school. They called her to bring clothing for my brother because he smelled. That's when she finally spoke up."

During the 1950s and 1960s, it took a lot of courage for a black mother to stand up for her children at a predominantly white school in a state that had earned a reputation for being racist, segregated, antiblack, and violent. But Nyala's mama was fed up with how her children were being treated by teachers. So on that day when she was notified that her son had defecated on himself, she grabbed an extra pair of clothing and marched down to the schoolhouse. She wanted to make something clear to the educators at that school: "Ain't nothing wrong with my children!" she announced. "They just learn slower." This mother wanted educators to stop viewing her children as individuals who weren't capable of learning and students who deserved to be mistreated by adults at school. What she did took a lot of courage, but her love for her children and her desire to see them get a decent education were stronger than any fear that the Jim Crow south had instilled in her.

When she recounted this story to me, Nyala didn't say how the school officials reacted to her mother's declaration. She did, however, explain how it affected her: It changed her self-concept. "I always knew that I wasn't dumb," she said. Despite the fact that she had begun to view herself as a "jackass" at school, deep down inside, she knew that she had the potential to be a good student. After all, at the all-black school, she had excelled at reading, and if she had been given a chance to read orally at the white school and improve her reading skills, perhaps she could have become one of the top readers in her class. Her mother's words to school officials on that day reminded her of something that she had once believed strongly: She wasn't dumb.

Even though her mother's words had reminded Nyala of her own potential, apparently they did little, if anything, to change the way that white teachers at her elementary school viewed her. They continued to view her as deficient, and the labels that they placed on her had dire consequences. When she completed elementary school and went to junior high school, Nyala was placed in a special education class.

Being placed in special education, especially as an older student rather than one in elementary school, could have resulted in several negative consequences for Nyala. She could have become so disillusioned that she eventually dropped out of school. She could have become a rebellious discipline problem who made the teacher's life a nightmare. She could have started believing that her mother was wrong and the teachers were right; perhaps she really was dumb after all. But in Nyala's case, being placed in special education turned out to be a huge blessing in disguise. And the main reason was the teacher.

Like most of her elementary school teachers, Nyala's seventh-grade teacher was a white woman. But this teacher had a different mindset about African American children. She believed in their ability to learn, and she used teaching strategies that reflected this belief. "She taught all of the subjects," Nyala said proudly. "That's when I finally caught up, because she taught at a slower pace. That's when I caught up in spelling and in reading." But more than anything, that seventh-grade teacher reawakened Nyala's belief in her potential to be a good student.

On the day that Nyala and I met, as we stood chatting in front of the elementary school where she worked, she remembered that seventh-grade teacher with great fondness and gratitude. One of the long-term consequences of this teacher's skill-development work with Nyala was that it permitted her to pursue her dream of becoming a sheriff's deputy. When she enrolled in the sheriff's academy, tackled the course work, and took exams, Nyala relied on some of the very strategies that the seventh-grade teacher had taught her. Later, when Nyala graduated and joined the sheriff's department, she knew that her fate might have been very different if she hadn't had that one special teacher—a white woman in Alabama who rose above the status quo in order to empower African American children by giving them a good education.

Many years later, Nyala retired from the sheriff's department and decided to work as a school security guard. Her current job is to protect the children and adults on campus from harm. She made it clear to me that just as she is concerned about their physical safety, she is equally as concerned about the quality of education that the children at the school are receiving. She realizes that even though her own K–12 school experiences occurred decades ago, during a different era, today, countless African American children still encounter teachers who think and behave like her former elementary school teachers at the predominantly white school did.

EXERCISE 1A: REFLECTING ON NYALA'S STORY

1. What are the three most important points that you learned from Nyala's story?

_____

_____

_____

2. In your opinion, how might Nyala's brother's accident in fifth grade affect his future school experiences and his attitude about school?

3. Describe your most embarrassing school-related experience, when it occurred, your age at the time, and how it affected you.

4. Before she was placed in a seventh-grade special education class, Nyala had had negative experiences with white teachers. In your opinion, what made her seventh-grade teacher—a white woman living in a notoriously racist environment—behave differently than Nyala's previous white teachers?

5. If you had been one of Nyala's elementary or middle school teachers, what do you *think* she would tell other people about you?

6. If you were one of Nyala's former teachers, what would you *want* her to say about you as she described the effect that you had on her?

7. How can Nyala's story help you to become a better educator of African American students?

★ ★ ★ ★ ★

As I said previously, one of the reasons I wanted to share Nyala's story with you is because it illustrates the fact that teachers wield enormous power over students. Teachers can encourage, motivate, and empower students enough to make them believe that the sky is the limit to what they can accomplish at school and in life. Teachers can also damage students to the point that students become apathetic about school and believe that they aren't capable of excelling academically. The next exercise will require you to think about your own K–12 school experiences and to describe the teachers who had a positive impact on you and those, if any, who had a negative one.

EXERCISE 1B: YOUR BEST AND WORST TEACHERS

Think back to your own K–12 school experiences.

1. How many outstanding, powerful, and life-changing teachers did you have?

   _____

   _____

2. Who were your outstanding elementary school teachers?

   _____

   _____

3. What qualities or characteristics made them outstanding?

   _____

   _____

4. Who were your outstanding middle school teachers?

   _____

   _____

5. What qualities or characteristics made them outstanding?

   _____

   _____

6. Who were your outstanding high school teachers?

   _____

   _____

7. What qualities or characteristics made them outstanding?

   _____

   _____

8. Now, review your answers to the first seven questions. What were the similarities among your best elementary, middle, and high school teachers?

_____

_____

9. How many negative, damaging, and/or uncaring K–12 teachers did you have?

_____

_____

10. Who were your worst elementary school teachers?

_____

_____

11. What qualities or characteristics made them bad teachers?

_____

_____

12. Who were your worst middle school teachers?

_____

_____

13. What qualities or characteristics made them bad teachers?

_____

_____

14. Who were your worst high school teachers?

_____

_____

15. What qualities or characteristics made them bad teachers?

_____

_____

16. Now, review your answers to the second set of questions. What were the similarities among your worst elementary, middle, and high school teachers?

_____

_____

17. What can you learn about good teachers from this exercise?

   _____

   _____

18. In terms of your own teaching efficacy, especially with African American students, how do you think you measure up to your best teachers?

   _____

   _____

19. In terms of your teaching efficacy, especially with African American students, how similar or different are you from your worst teachers?

   _____

   _____

20. In your opinion, what made your outstanding teachers decide to become good teachers?

   _____

   _____

21. In your opinion, what made your worst teachers decide to become bad teachers?

   _____

   _____

★   ★   ★   ★   ★

I hope that you had numerous outstanding K–12 teachers and few, if any, bad ones. Unfortunately, researchers have found that high-achieving students tend to report that they had more influential teachers than low-achievers report.[1] However, both groups report a dismally small number: less than two for low-achievers and about three for high-achievers.[2] It is a sad commentary on our educational system. In fact, often, when I ask educators, parents, and other individuals who attend my workshops how many powerful, influential, life-changing K–12 teachers they had, many indicate that they didn't even have *one*. In other words, during their entire K–12 education, not one teacher made a positive impact on them.

One of the questions that I have wondered about for a long time is, "Why do some teachers make a choice to be effective and others choose to be ineffective?" Of course, some ineffective teachers don't even realize that they are ineffective and never make a conscious decision to become so. Nevertheless, ineffective teachers damage students. Having several bad teachers in a row can be extremely detrimental to students because teachers are the most important in-school factor that affects student achievement.[3] The question of why some teachers choose to become ineffective has been on my mind for a long time, especially in regard to ineffective teachers of African American students. I wonder if they started out being idealistic and optimistic and then lost their zeal over time. Did discipline problems cause them to lose their desire to reach all students? Was it burnout? Did they become hopeless about their ability to truly help African American students succeed at school?

MY THEORY ABOUT INEFFECTIVE
TEACHERS OF AFRICAN AMERICAN STUDENTS

The question of why some teachers knowingly or unknowingly choose to become ineffective with African American students led me to formulate a theory: I believe that many teachers may subconsciously or consciously *choose* to become ineffective with African American students because they don't see the *payoffs—the personal benefits*—for themselves. After all, most people have to have a motive for the actions that they take. Let me explain what I mean by sharing a related personal example.

Have you ever gotten the bright idea to start a new diet, a new exercise regimen, a new hobby, a new class, or some other endeavor? If so, like most of us, you probably had a lot of enthusiasm and determination—at least at the beginning. But before long, you might have found that your enthusiasm was slowly—or maybe even quickly—disappearing. When this occurred, you had two choices—to stick to your plan anyway, or to throw in the towel and quit. Chances are that you were more likely to hang in there and reach that goal if you could convince yourself that the goal was worth achieving. If you had a fan club, or group of strong supporters, to encourage and cheer you on, the attainment of that goal probably became much easier. I had a similar experience many years ago during my quest to earn a doctorate.

At the time when I decided to go back to school, I was a teacher at a predominantly Latino, underperforming high school. I was married, and I had three school-age children. Upon hearing of my plans, one of my colleagues laughed in my face and implied that I was crazy. Others merely laughed behind my back and waited for me to fail. One extended family member told me that I was probably wasting my time.

In spite of this negativity, I enrolled in a local doctoral program and embarked on what I expected to be an adventurous educational journey. One semester later, I was bleary-eyed, sleep-deprived, and feeling that the naysayers may have been correct. This *was* crazy, and I didn't need the extra work and stress added to an already hectic life. So I decided to quit. To my surprise, a group of cheerleaders—my husband, my children, and a few friends—told me that I couldn't quit. And when they finished rattling off all of the ways in which I would benefit from finishing what I'd started, they had convinced me that I should remain in school. Their belief in me and their words of encouragement gave me the fuel that I needed to stay on course. However, each semester they had to "refuel" me. In the end, I earned the doctorate, and I am grateful that my family and friends were instrumental in helping me to keep the personal benefits in mind each time that I seriously considered quitting.

Even though I often thought about quitting school during that time, the *personal benefits* of earning a doctorate were always clear to me. First, earning the doctorate would qualify me to apply for tenure-track teaching positions at colleges and universities. Second, earning the doctorate would permit me to have more time to pursue research projects that interested me. Third, I would have time to write the books that I never seemed to have enough time to write. Fourth, I would be in a position to share what I had learned with educators by conducting workshops and presenting my work at conferences.

Conversely, in the case of teachers who choose to become ineffective, I wonder if they have either forgotten or have never known how they can benefit personally from being excellent educators of African American students. The theory that I developed led me to create a simple question-naire called the "What's In It for Me?" questionnaire. Before I tell you more about what I learned from distributing this questionnaire to a group of educators, I would like you to complete the following exercise.

EXERCISE 1C: IDENTIFYING THE PERSONAL BENEFITS OF BEING AN EFFECTIVE EDUCATOR OF AFRICAN AMERICAN STUDENTS

1. How would you rate your level of effectiveness with any African American students that you currently have or with those with whom you have worked in the past?

_____

_____

2. What specific examples can you provide to justify the rating that you gave yourself?

_____

_____

3. List at least three ways in which you would personally benefit from becoming a better educator of African American students.

_____

_____

_____

★ ★ ★ ★ ★

Hopefully, you were able to complete the previous exercise without too much difficulty. I also hope that you were able to think of at least three ways that you would personally benefit from increasing your efficacy with African American students. In the next section, you will read about how another group of educators responded to a similar exercise. As you're reading their responses, compare and contrast your responses with theirs. Then, go back to your list and add any new benefits that you hadn't already thought of.

THE "WHAT'S IN IT FOR ME?" QUESTIONNAIRE RESULTS

In March 2008, I gave a presentation to 108 educators and individuals who were affiliated with Minnesota schools in some capacity. More than half of the participants were white, and 32% were black. Although only 12% of the participants were currently working as classroom teachers, 64% had worked as educators in one capacity or another. In fact, 60% had been educators for at least five years, and nearly 30% had been educators for more than 20 years (see Appendix A for more information about the conference participants). Most were currently working as specialists who trained teachers to better serve a multiethnic student body.

At the beginning of the presentation, I asked the participants to complete the "What's In It for Me?" questionnaire that I had developed. In addition to providing background information about their age group, job, and race or ethnicity, participants were instructed to "List three ways in which you would *personally* benefit from working more effectively with black students." The two most frequently cited answers were "It will benefit society and/or the community," and "I would understand students and their parents better." The next most frequently cited answer was "I would feel better about myself." One fourth of the respondents said, "I would become a better teacher," 20% said that "It would improve students' futures," and 20% said "I will have better relations with these students." Less than 10% of the participants said that becoming a more effective educator of African American students would "decrease discipline problems," "improve students' skills," or "improve test scores." (See Appendix B for more information about the participants' responses.)

The personal benefits that the conference participants cited can be grouped into two main categories: those that would directly benefit the educators, and those that would indirectly benefit them. For example, the participants who said that becoming more effective educators of African American students would benefit society and the community were citing ways in which the educators would benefit indirectly. As members of society, these educators realized that if they provided their African American students with a quality education, it could be a win-win situation: A good education increases the likelihood that the students will grow up to become hardworking, law-abiding adults instead of becoming a financial drain on taxpayers by getting caught in the "prison pipeline" or stuck in an endless cycle of poverty. Similarly, respondents who said that becoming more effective with African American students would benefit the educators by "improving students' futures" were also citing an indirect and long-term benefit. By providing African American students with a quality education, they could position students to pursue their dreams of getting good jobs and/or attending college. In Nyala's case, her seventh-grade teacher's hard work enabled Nyala to pursue her dream of enrolling in the sheriff's academy and to eventually get the job of her dream. Evidently, the educators who cited long-term indirect benefits might have had a mindset that was similar to that of Nyala's teacher.

Four of the six most commonly cited personal benefits were direct benefits. Educators who said that increasing their efficacy with African American students would "help them better understand students and parents" and those who said it would permit them to have "better relations with these students" could utilize what they learned immediately and, thereby, improve their pedagogy and relations with African American students and parents. Respondents who said that increasing their efficacy would "help them feel better about themselves" were alluding to the well-known adage "When I do good, I feel good." Knowing that they were working effectively with African American students might help them to sleep better at night because they were not choosing to shortchange students academically or perpetuate inequality of educational opportunity in the way that some of Nyala's elementary school teachers did. Another direct benefit, that of "improving my teaching," could clearly benefit teachers directly, swiftly, and on a short-term and long-term basis. Obviously, the respondents who cited this benefit realized what so many researchers—including myself—have tried to tell educators for years: "If you become an outstanding teacher of African American students, all students will benefit!" Moreover, teachers who choose to do this will develop better and more effective teaching skills.

Both categories of responses consisted of *intrinsic rewards*, nonmonetary rewards. In fact, researchers have found that "teachers are motivated more by intrinsic than by extrinsic rewards," and many teachers "are primarily motivated by intrinsic rewards such as self-respect, responsibility, and a sense of accomplishment."[4] Hopefully, your responses to Exercise 1C also reflect that you are mainly motivated by intrinsic rewards in order to make a lifelong positive impact on *all* of your students, including the African Americans.

POINTS TO KEEP IN MIND

The main point that I would like you to remember after reading Nyala's story and completing the exercises in this chapter is that, as an educator, you will make some type of impact on students. The questions to always keep in mind are "Am I making the type of impact that I want to make?" and "Am I making the type of impact that I will be proud of in the long run?" The book *Who Mentored You? The Person Who Changed My Life: Prominent People Recall Their Mentors*[5] is a good example of what I'm saying.

The book consists of stories that 40 well-known individuals shared about the people who contributed to their success. Twenty-one of the celebrities, including three African Americans—the late actor Ossie Davis, the actor James Earl Jones, and the singer Jessye Norman—mentioned that one or more of their K–12 school teachers had made a lasting, positive impact on them. In fact, nearly 30 teachers were mentioned in the book. These celebrities told poignant stories about the specific ways in which various teachers had helped them to overcome difficulties, empowered them, and played a role in their success.

However, as I was skimming the book, I couldn't help but notice that many of the celebrities—including six African Americans—never said that even one teacher had made a positive impact on them. I wondered whether, if given the chance, these celebrities would have shared horrific stories about teachers who might have actually damaged them or, at the very least, underestimated their potential. The fact that so many of them couldn't even say that one teacher had contributed to their success should remind us of two very important points: (1) It is possible to overlook greatness in students without realizing it, and (2) one day, we may regret that we didn't go out of our way to try to reach certain students. Today, for example, I wonder how many former K–12 teachers of the celebrities in the book wished that those very same celebrities would mention their names in an acceptance speech. On the other hand, how many teachers beamed with pride when they saw their names cited in the book *Who Mentored You?* because their former students wanted the world to know what phenomenal teachers they were? What a wonderful *personal benefit* to receive so many years after they *chose* to become outstanding educators.

Although the theme of this chapter is that there are personal benefits in choosing to become an outstanding educator of African American students, I hope you will also remember the following points:

- Even when the personal benefits aren't obvious to you, all students—including African Americans—deserve an outstanding education.
- Sometimes, you might not ever see the fruit of your labor: how well the students that you have invested so much time and energy into turned out as adults.
- There are direct benefits for you in choosing to become an outstanding educator of African American students.
- There are indirect benefits for you in choosing to become an outstanding educator of African American students.
- Many years after you have chosen to become an outstanding educator of African American students, you might receive an unexpected confirmation that your hard work wasn't done in vain.

Let me illustrate this last point by sharing another short, personal story with you. During the summer of 2008, I received an e-mail that underscored the message that I'm trying to convey to you in this chapter. One of my former high school students, an African American male, e-mailed me in order to thank me for all of my hard work on his behalf. Throughout the years, I had often wondered how he was doing and prayed that he had turned out well. So when I received the e-mail, I couldn't wait to speak with him by telephone.

A few days later, the much-anticipated telephone conversation occurred. He told me that he was raising his two young sons and was engaged to marry a wonderful woman. Although he had gone through a difficult divorce, he wanted to make sure that his sons had a supportive family and developed good academic skills. As I listened to him describe his life, tears formed in my eyes because I remembered how difficult his high school years had been as a result of problems in his home life. Nevertheless, I and several other teachers had tried to mentor him, and I encouraged him to use education as a means of improving his future. Apparently, our hard work paid off; when we spoke by telephone, he was close to finishing the requirements to earn his master's degree! He had also been instrumental in encouraging his younger brother to attend college, and he had big plans for his sons.

At the end of the conversation, I reflected on how well this young man had turned out. I was grateful to God that the work and effort that I and several other high school teachers invested in him had paid off so well and that I had been blessed enough to hear the good news about his progress. Although I invested the same amount of energy, time, and effort into countless other K–12 students, I will probably never hear "thank yous" or updates from them. That's just a fact of life. However, even though I will never hear from most of them, the bottom line for me is that I know that I tried to do my very best—in spite of the many mistakes that I made along the way. The fact that I tried to make a positive impact on my former students makes me feel good about the work that I've done. In other words, I'm still reaping a personal benefit—an intrinsic reward—in the form of feeling good about how I *chose* to use my time in the classroom and the power that I had as a teacher.

In the chapters that follow, you will read stories about other educators who chose or chose not to become outstanding educators of African American students, and the related consequences. But before you read the next chapter, please complete one final exercise that I designed to help you remember the main points of this chapter.

EXERCISE 1D: UPDATING YOUR "WHAT'S IN IT FOR ME?" LIST

1. Now that you have read Chapter 1, review the list that you wrote for Exercise 1C. Rewrite the list below, and then, add additional ways that you would personally benefit from increasing your efficacy with African American students.

   a.

   b.

   c.

   d.

   e.

   f.

   Whenever you feel like quitting, or feel that your work is in vain, or that you aren't making any progress with your African American students, revisit the list that you wrote for Exercise 1D. Then, think of the positive experiences that you have had with one or more African American students, and refuel yourself. Seeking support from others can also be helpful. The next section can help you do this.

2. Make a list of individuals who can become your own personal cheerleaders during the times when you feel discouraged. This list can include positive family members, effective teachers of African American students, supportive administrators, mentor teachers, and others.

   a.

   b.

   c.

   d.

   e.

3. On New Year's Day 2008, one of my former graduate students died at age 47. For several years, this African American mother of four, high school teacher, and track coach had battled ovarian cancer. One week after she died, I spoke at her funeral about the positive impact that she'd had on me. After returning to my seat in the crowded Baptist church, I listened as speaker after speaker spoke about the ways in which she had affected their lives. The stories that resonated with me the most were those shared by several of her former high school students. If several of your African American students attended your *homegoing* (a euphemism for "funeral" that is used in many black churches), what would you want them to say about you?

   _____

   _____

4. Based on what you learned from this chapter, what, if any, changes do you need to make in order to become the type of educator whom your African American students will speak well of and remember with fondness, respect, and gratitude?

_____

_____

GROUP ACTIVITY FOR PROFESSIONAL DEVELOPMENT AND COURSE WORK

1. Ask 10 administrators and teachers at your school site or at a local K–12 school, "What are the personal benefits of becoming a better educator of African American students?"

2. Analyze their responses.

3. Compare and contrast their responses with your own.

4. Explain to the rest of the group what you learned from this activity.

5. As a group, determine how you can use this information to empower educators at the participating schools.

2

That Baggage Is Too Heavy

Uncovering Negative Mindsets That Can Undermine Your Work With African American Students

Traveling by air is a lot more stressful than it used to be. Ticket prices are ridiculously high. Getting through security is a headache. Planes are often delayed and overbooked, and flights are even cancelled with little or no forewarning to passengers. Some airlines are even charging passengers for items that used to be free, such as water, soft drinks, snacks, blankets, and pillows. On top of all of this, there's the problem of baggage. Several airlines have placed serious limitations on the number, size, and weight of both carry-on and checked luggage, and some airlines penalize passengers who check one or more bags. Therefore, baggage can be a problem! The kind of baggage that I'll be referring to in the remainder of this chapter is of a different type—personal baggage—which can impede your progress with African American students.

Psychologist Beth McHugh defines *personal baggage* as simply "all the things that aren't right in your life."[1] For example, as a woman who has struggled with my weight for much of my adult life, my personal baggage sometimes includes a gut that is too big for me to fit into some of the clothes in my closet. This type of personal baggage is common in the United States; many of us are overweight. Through exercise, controlling the amount of food that we eat, and awareness, we can get rid of this baggage problem.

Another type of personal baggage is what the rest of this chapter will focus on: mental baggage. The mental baggage that I'm specifically referring to consists of negative, biased, stereotypical, or deficit mindsets that will, undoubtedly, hinder your progress with African American students. But before I continue, please answer the following question as honestly as you can.

EXERCISE 2A: YOUR PERSPECTIVE ON AFRICAN AMERICAN STUDENTS

When you think about most African American K–12 students, what comes to mind? (Circle any of the following answers that apply, and feel free to write in other responses.)

(a) pathology   (b) children from broken and dysfunctional homes

(c) children who have uncaring parents (d) future gang members

(e) future prison inmates   (f) future welfare recipients or low-wage earners

(g) other _____

Or do you see

(a) brilliance   (b) great potential   (c) future doctors   (d) future attorneys

(e) future professors   (f) future congressmen and women   (g) future judges

(h) future presidential candidates   (i) song composers   (j) film makers

(k) authors   (l) other _____

I asked you this question because researchers have found that what we believe can become a self-fulfilling prophecy in the classroom. Our beliefs can affect the ways in which we view and treat students, the quality of education we provide them, and our expectations of their potential.[2] Therefore, in order to truly become more effective with African American students, you must be *willing* to face your mental baggage about them, you must be *honest* with yourself, and you must be *courageous* enough to get rid of your negative beliefs. As you'll see in the next section, this isn't as easy as it sounds.

WHAT MANY EDUCATORS BELIEVE ABOUT AFRICAN AMERICAN STUDENTS

Most of us are familiar with the old saying, "Honesty is the best policy." Do you believe this? Here's a harder question: Can you *honestly* express your beliefs about African American students? The next exercise is designed to determine if you can.

EXERCISE 2B: SPECIFIC VIEWS ABOUT AFRICAN AMERICAN STUDENTS AND PARENTS

Read each statement. Circle "True" if you believe that the statement is true, or "False" if you believe it is false.

1. I honestly believe that my African American students are capable of doing outstanding academic work.   True   False

2. I honestly believe that most of my African American students have caring parents or guardians.   True   False

3. I am just as confident about my ability to help my African American students do well in my class(es) as I am about my ability to help my other students.   True   False

4. To be honest, I would prefer not to deal with African American students.   True   False

5. I truly believe that most of my African American students are just as smart as most of my other students.   True   False

6. Now, review your answers. Did you respond to each statement honestly?
   Yes ___   No ___

7. If not, why didn't you do so?

   _____

8. If you did respond to each statement honestly, what can you learn from your responses?

   _____

I hope that you were courageous enough to respond to each statement honestly. But if you're like many educators, you may have had trouble honestly expressing your views about African American students. I learned this in 2007, after I conducted a workshop for teachers and administrators at an elementary school in southern California.

At the beginning of the workshop, I asked the 71 participants to respond to the same set of statements to which you just responded. I did this because I wanted to learn about their self-described views and treatment of African American students.

Later, as I was analyzing the data, I noticed an interesting pattern: Almost all of the educators gave what they *thought* were the politically correct answers. In other words, most of the educators said that they treated their African American students fairly and that they believed that African American students were just as smart as other students (see Appendix C).

THE MINDSET STUDY

So I decided to change my approach. I created a survey called "The Mindset Questionnaire" in order to give respondents an opportunity to express their views about how educators *in general* treat and perceive African American students. Based on what had happened with the educators at the elementary school, I assumed that most respondents would be more honest about replying to statements pertaining to educators *in general,* instead of having to express their own views about black students. After analyzing questionnaire data from 143 educators in Texas and 94 preservice teachers in California who attended workshops that I conducted in those states, I learned some startling information. (See Appendix D for demographic information about these respondents.)

For me, the most surprising finding was that the overwhelming majority of respondents in *all* subgroups (administrators, teachers, preservice teachers, whites, nonwhites, males, and females) said that most teachers *don't know* how to work effectively with African American K–12 students. Ninety percent of the preservice teachers, 94% of the teachers, and nearly all (98%) of the black respondents indicated this. (See Appendix E for more information.)

The respondents also expressed their views about the underachievement of many black K–12 students. Most blamed *school factors* rather than *nonschool factors.* The main school factor that they identified was low teacher expectations, which correlates to what many researchers have been saying for years.[3] This is an important finding because researchers have found that low teacher expectations can become a self-fulfilling prophecy in the classroom, that they may play a large role in the black-nonblack achievement gaps, and that African American students tend to perform better academically in a culture that is based on high expectations.[4] A substantial percentage of participants also blamed poor teaching methods and a nonculturally relevant curriculum for black students' underachievement—problems that experts have attempted to tackle for years.[5]

Two other disturbing findings pertained to what the respondents said about students' intelligence and their capabilities. With the exception of males and whites, half or more than half (50%–75%) of each subgroup indicated that most teachers don't believe that African American students are as intelligent as nonblacks. The majority of the respondents also indicated that most teachers and school principals don't believe that most African American K–12 students are capable of academic excellence. Researchers have also tried to bring attention to the problem of deficit mindsets and related consequences for years.[6]

The questionnaire item about teachers' views and treatment of African American students garnered more negative responses than any other statement. The overwhelming majority (66%–98%) of preservice teachers, teachers, administrators, whites, nonwhites, males, and females said that most teachers don't treat and view African American students in the same ways that they do nonblacks. Despite the fact that many teachers claim to be "colorblind" to racial differences,[7] researchers have found that, often, the student's race determines how his or her teacher will treat the student.[8]

I'll discuss some of the other findings from the Mindset Study later. Now, I would like you to spend some time reflecting on what you learned from the questionnaire results that I just described.

EXERCISE 2C: REFLECTING ON THE MINDSET STUDY RESULTS

Please answer each of the following questions as honestly as possible.

1. Which Mindset Study results surprised you the most, and why?

   _____

   _____

2. Which results were least surprising to you, and why?

   _____

   _____

3. What did you learn from the results of the Mindset Study?

   _____

   _____

4. What are the similarities and differences between your own responses to the Mindset Study (Exercise 2B) and the responses of the Texas and California respondents?

   _____

   _____

5. How can you use the information that you learned from the study to become a better educator of African American students?

_____

_____

HOW EDUCATORS' NEGATIVE MINDSETS CAN HARM STUDENTS

I began this chapter by defining negative mindsets as mental baggage that we carry. Of course, in this book, my big concern is specifically about mental baggage that can impede your progress with African American students. But we also need to look at why it is so important for you to not only identify but also to "unload" this mental baggage. I'll illustrate this by telling you a story that an African American male, who lives in Chicago, shared with me by telephone.

One day, during fall 2007, I arrived at my office at the university to find a voicemail awaiting me. The male caller stated that he had recently seen me on *Tony Brown's Journal* (a public television program that had rebroadcast an interview with me) and needed to speak with me. I returned the call, only to get his answering machine. So I left a message and informed him of the best times for him to reach me in my office. That was the beginning of several days of "phone tag."

After receiving other voicemail messages from him that were left on days when I hadn't said that I'd be in my office, I became frustrated. "Why doesn't he simply state the reason why he's calling?" I wondered. Finally, I decided that I'd return his call one last time, and if I didn't reach him, I wouldn't attempt to call him again. But when I made that last call, the story that the man (whom I'll refer to as "Nathan") shared made me forever grateful that I reached him. The story that he told broke my heart, and as he recounted it, both of us wept periodically. Nathan said that he wanted me to hear his story so that I would share it with a larger audience. Now, I'm sharing it with you—the reader—because it emphasizes how important it is for educators, including yourself, to deal with your mental baggage about African American children.

NATHAN'S STORY: "THEY DESTROYED MY DESIRE TO LEARN IN THEIR SCHOOLS."

Nathan's story actually began long before he was born. As a child, his father, an extremely light-skinned black boy from Alabama, was such a high achiever that he was able to go north to attend Phillips Academy in

Andover, Massachusetts. Today, "Andover," a prestigious boarding high school that was founded in 1778, still has a good reputation. In 1789, President George Washington gave a speech at the school when he went there to visit his nephew, a student at the school.[9] "Andover's 1778 Constitution charges the academy to prepare 'youth from every quarter' to understand that 'goodness without knowledge is weak . . . yet knowledge without goodness is dangerous.'"[10] This charge, undoubtedly, had a lasting effect on Nathan's father.

After Andover, he attended prestigious universities and eventually became a surgeon who was committed to helping poor African Americans in Chicago receive good healthcare. "Dad was a humanitarian," Nathan said. "He gave free healthcare. He didn't care about money. All he cared about was people." Because Nathan's father cared more about helping low-income people than about becoming wealthy, he and his family—his wife, a registered pediatric nurse, and two sons—remained on the south side of Chicago throughout his entire medical career. In spite of their financial struggles, both he and his wife instilled a strong love for learning in Nathan and his younger brother. According to Nathan:

> My dad—God rest his soul—is my hero. . . . My mom too. My dad—what he achieved educationally—we are all so proud of him. He was a king of a daddy. Daddy was always keen on learning and I was too. Everyone always thought that I would follow in his footsteps. I was like the spitting image of him.

In addition to teaching Nathan how to read before he started school, Nathan's father, who spoke eight different languages, also taught him how to speak several languages, starting when Nathan was four years old. In fact, Nathan's parents believed so strongly in the value of a good education that they decided to enroll their sons in Catholic schools. Because Nathan's mother was a devout Catholic, she and her husband believed that their children would get a better education in Catholic schools.

So when Nathan, a little black boy from the south side of Chicago, started elementary school, he was excited about learning more than he already knew. But almost from the beginning, problems surfaced. He attended a predominantly-black Catholic elementary school, and all of his teachers were white priests and nuns who, ironically, were called "Sisters of Mercy." According to Nathan, "It started in primary school with all these nuns and priests who were jealous of my dad." The "it" that he was referring to was racism. As a young child, he saw subtle manifestations of it at school. "They didn't care about us," Nathan remarked, "but we were probably getting a better education than the black kids in the public school system." In spite of this realization, Nathan continued to excel academically. But when he reached middle school, the racism intensified, and what happened during eighth grade changed the course of his life.

At the predominantly black, prestigious Catholic school that Nathan attended, the students were segregated by gender during eighth grade. Therefore, on the first day of school, Nathan found himself in a classroom full of black boys. On top of this, he learned that he and his classmates would only have one teacher that year—Sister Mary P. (I am choosing not to include her last name in this book)—a nun who would teach all of the subjects.

On the first day of school, Sister Mary P. introduced herself to the class in a way that Nathan would never forget: "I know a lot of you. I know you are low-life people." According to Nathan, Sister Mary P. "looked at us like we were all sons of criminals, or like we didn't know who our dads were. This is how she introduced herself to us. . . . It went downhill from there. She would tell us that we're all low-lifes, so when she found out my daddy was a doctor, that killed her. Not to mention that daddy had light skin and blue eyes!"

In spite of this frightening introduction by Sister Mary P., Nathan continued to be the child that his parents had trained him to be—a student who was serious about his education and loved to learn. But it was this very attitude about learning that would soon contribute to his demise as a student.

The incident that made Nathan utter loud, gut-wrenching sobs during our telephone conversation occurred on the day before his eighth-grade class was scheduled to take a national Catholic high school entrance exam. This test would determine which high school he would be able to attend the following year. After finishing his class work early, Nathan began to read ahead in one of his textbooks. "I just loved learning. I was an over-achiever," he explained. "I was so ahead of the class, and she [Sister Mary P.] didn't like any one of us. She didn't appreciate [his reading ahead in the textbook], and then, knowing that dad and mom were who they were—jealously—she didn't appreciate it."

As he sat at his desk silently reading the textbook, Nathan wasn't prepared for what happened next. Sister Mary P. walked over to him and declared, "So you went ahead!" Then, using one of her hands, she back-handed him in his left eye. "She was angry," Nathan explained, "because I went ahead in my lessons." Although he was astonished, Nathan shouldn't have been, for this was actually the second time that Sister Mary P. had hit him in the same eye. "Thank God, she didn't hit me with an object," he told me. "But she would use objects to hit us with—paddles with holes in them. She would use sticks—pointer sticks—that she would often beat us with. She would [also] use her fists. She was very physically abusive."

After school ended that day, by the time he arrived home, Nathan's left eye was swollen shut. He told his parents what had happened, "And they were so passive," he said. "They didn't essentially say anything. I was made to go to school the following morning with one eye shut."

After all, he couldn't miss the national exam that was so important to his academic future.

During the exam, Nathan struggled to read the questions. Although he had studied, because he could only see out of one eye, it took longer for him to complete the exam. "I did just good enough to pass," he remarked sadly. "But I could've done better. I had trouble seeing. I had one eye swollen shut. I was so badly injured that I couldn't see out of it the next morning. I passed [the exam] but I scored low, not because I didn't know the answers, but because I was so slow [in completing the exam]."

What Sister Mary P. did on that day when she backhanded Nathan for the second time left him partially blind for the rest of his life. But she had also damaged his self-esteem to the point that he went from being a high-achieving student who loved learning to a student who began to hate the education system. "They destroyed my desire to learn in their schools," he sobbed. "This nun was absolutely merciless. It's ironic that they're called the Sisters of Mercy. . . . The younger you are when they get you, the more they influence you in a bad or a good way."

The last straw occurred when Nathan was 14 years old, during the summer before he became a high school sophomore. He had already become disillusioned with the Catholic School system, and on top of this, he was getting very little sleep at night. Because his father was elderly, Nathan and his brother accompanied him on his house calls. "We should've gone to Andover," he explained, "but Dad needed us. We often went on my dad's rounds with him late at night. So we never got any sleep."

One night that summer, thieves attacked Nathan's father during a house call. "Desperate people do desperate things," he explained sadly. The robbers "beat him to a pulp. He was so old. Dad was like 75. They crushed his skull and everything." Although Nathan's father tried to continue practicing medicine, he never fully recovered from the brutal beating. In fact, things had worsened to the point that Nathan had to change his father's diapers when he arrived home from high school each day.

By his sophomore year of high school, Nathan had basically given up on school. "I had to change diapers on Daddy," he stated. "This is what I couldn't share with my high school peers, [yet] I had to keep up with my high school peers [academically.]" Regarding school, he explained, "I felt that I just didn't care. My heart wasn't there. All the while, I'm changing diapers. Dad was just getting worse."

Nathan eventually graduated from high school. Although he attended college, he had lost his motivation to succeed academically. Before long, he "entered the world of drugs," and "just drifted from one college to another. I didn't obtain any degree," he stated. For 20 years, he smoked marijuana and was hooked on cocaine. However, in 1989, after deciding to change his life, he got off of drugs.

Today, he is the father and sole-caretaker of his physically disabled adult daughter, whose mother died of cancer when the child was 11 years old. "I encourage her to do more with her life," Nathan said of his daughter. And although Nathan insists that he still despises the education system, his dream of earning a college degree—a dream that his parents instilled in him before he even began attending kindergarten—has not died. "The only thing is," he said as he burst into tears again, "they destroyed my desire to learn in their system. They destroyed my desire to learn in their schools, and I'm trying to recover from that. It's hard for me to be in class and take notes." Despite the fact that Nathan isn't sure if his dream of earning a college degree will ever come true, the thirst for knowledge and love of learning that his parents gave to him remain. "I keep wanting to learn," he said. "I'm an avid reader. It's in my DNA. I can't help it. They [the nuns and priests] couldn't kill that."

EXERCISE 2D: REFLECTING ON NATHAN'S STORY

Please respond to each of the following questions as honestly as possible.

1. What are your overall thoughts about Nathan's story?

   _____

   _____

2. What are the main messages that you learned from this story?

   _____

   _____

3. How does this story pertain to mindsets?

   _____

   _____

★　★　★　★　★

WHY SISTER MARY P. NEEDED BRAIN SURGERY

One of the main reasons I wanted to share Nathan's story with you is so that you could see the connection between thoughts and actions. For some reason, Sister Mary P. had formed a very negative opinion of the black boys in her class; on the first day of school, she made several negative remarks about them. Even after she learned that she had the high-achieving son of a surgeon and a registered pediatric nurse in her class, her actions indicated that she still had a negative view of Nathan and his classmates. In my opinion, Sister Mary P. needed brain surgery. Of course, when I say that "Sister Mary P. needed brain surgery," I'm speaking figuratively. What she really needed was the eradication of her negative beliefs—her mental baggage—about black boys. That baggage was weighing her down, harming her students, and keeping her from being an effective and fair instructor of the children whom she was being paid to educate. This brings us to two obvious questions: (1) Can negative mindsets be changed? (2) If negative mindsets can be changed, how can it been done? Before we look more closely at these questions, please take a moment to complete the following exercise.

EXERCISE 2E: YOUR BELIEFS ABOUT NEGATIVE MINDSETS

Please respond to each of the following questions as honestly as possible.

1. Do you believe that negative mindsets can be changed? Why or why not?

   _____

   _____

2. Which negative mindsets are easiest to change and why?

   _____

   _____

3. Which negative mindsets are hardest to change and why?

   _____

   _____

★   ★   ★   ★   ★

CAN NEGATIVE MINDSETS BE CHANGED?

There are two reasons why I hope that you said "Yes, it is possible for negative mindsets to be changed." First, I want you to be *hopeful* about the possibility of change. Second, and more important, I want you to be hopeful about the possibility of changing any of your own negative mindsets, beliefs, mental baggage, and so on that can prevent you from being an outstanding educator of African American students. Now, let's look specifically at what other educators believe about whether or not it's possible for educators to change their negative mindsets about African American students.

During the summer of 2007, I conducted professional development workshops at two very different schools and asked the 69 participants to complete two questionnaires. One of the workshops was held at a public elementary school in Los Angeles County, and the other was held at a private college preparatory high school in Los Angeles County (see Appendix F for demographic information about the workshop participants). Now, I want to tell you about the "Searching for Solutions" questionnaire because some of the questions pertain specifically to educators' negative mindsets about African American students.

When asked "In your opinion, is it possible for educators to change negative mindsets and stereotypes that they have about African American students," 91% of the workshop participants said "yes." Hopefully, when you completed Exercise 2E, you said the same thing, for as you'll see in the next section, experts agree that it is possible for people to make major changes in the way that they think.

WHAT EXPERTS SAY

According to Dr. Derald Wing Sue, an author, educator, and expert on racism:

- It is difficult, but possible, for us to get rid of our stereotypes about others, even when we receive logical information to refute the stereotypes, or even when we have experiences that counter our stereotypical beliefs.
- Harboring negative stereotypes about others can make us feel better about ourselves.
- Because our identity is linked to the stereotypes that we hold about others, we may become defensive when our stereotypes are challenged.
- In order to prevent their stereotypes from being challenged, some people resort to various tactics, such as avoidance and "psychological maneuvers."[11]

In his book, *Changing Minds: The Art and Science of Changing Our Own and Other People's Minds*, Howard Gardner, a psychologist, former teacher, and author, reached several interesting conclusions about mind changing. According to Gardner:

- It is easier for children to change their minds than adults.
- When mind changing occurs, the result is also a change in behavior.
- It is difficult for people to change their minds about issues to which they are emotionally attached.

- People who have publicly stated their beliefs about various issues are less likely to change their minds about those issues for the sake of pride.
- People with more "flexible" personalities are more likely to change than those with rigid, "authoritarian personalities."[12]

HOW CAN NEGATIVE MINDSETS BE CHANGED?

Now that it's clear that it is possible, though difficult, to change negative mindsets, the most logical next question is "How can negative mindsets be changed?" The 69 workshop participants who completed the "Searching for Solutions" questionnaire shared their thoughts about this topic. Five main themes emerged from their responses. According to the workshop participants, in order to change their negative mindsets about African American students, educators need to

- increase their education and awareness (57%);
- face their biases, identify stereotypes, and engage in introspection (41%);
- make a personal commitment to change negative beliefs (23%);
- use the community, students, and parents as resources (16%); and
- improve their own behavior and classroom practices (15%).

ARE YOU READY AND WILLING TO CHANGE?

Throughout this chapter, I have emphasized three main points: (1) Many educators have negative mindsets—mental baggage—about African American students; (2) in order to increase your efficacy with African American students, you must be willing to face any negative mental baggage that you have about them; and (3) you must be willing to do what's necessary to get rid of this baggage. I designed the next section in order to help you begin the process of facing and ridding yourself of this baggage.

EXERCISE 2F: FACING YOUR BAGGAGE ABOUT AFRICAN AMERICANS

Please respond to each of the following questions as honestly as possible.

1. When you were growing up, what did your parents or guardians teach you about African Americans?

_____

_____

2. When you were growing up, what did your friends teach you about African Americans?

_____

_____

3. When you were growing up, what did the media teach you about African Americans?

_____

_____

4. When you were growing up, what did your teachers teach you about African Americans?

_____

_____

5. When you were growing up, what did your religious leader(s) teach you about African Americans?

_____

_____

6. When you were growing up, what did you learn about African Americans from direct contact with them?

_____

_____

7. Now review your answers to Questions 1 through 6, and explain which, if any, of the views that you formed about Africans Americans during childhood have changed.

_____

_____

8. When you think of African American K–12 students, what are your main thoughts about African American females?

_____

_____

9. When you think of African American K–12 students, what are your main thoughts about African American males?

_____

_____

10. Now, please review your answers to Questions 1 through 9. Explain how your beliefs can help or harm your African American students.

_____

_____

11. In your opinion, what impact will changing your beliefs about African American students have on your teaching efficacy?

_____

_____

12. What, if any, concerns, fears, or reservations do you have about changing your beliefs about African American students?

_____

_____

13. Who or what could help you to alleviate the aforementioned fears, reservations, or concerns, and are you willing to utilize this resource or individual in order to move forward with your professional development work?

_____

_____

★   ★   ★   ★   ★

MOVING FORWARD

The previous exercise required you to engage in honest self-reflection about the messages that you internalized during childhood about African Americans. It also encouraged you to examine your current views about African American students. This honest self-reflection is an important step in the process that can help you rid yourself of this mental baggage in order to increase your teaching efficacy. The method that I recommend for ridding yourself of this baggage is based on *cognitive restructuring*.

WHAT IS COGNITIVE RESTRUCTURING?

According to Drs. Mark Dombeck and Jolyn Wells-Moran, cognitive restructuring (sometimes known as *reframing*) is a technique that "is designed to help you alter your habitual appraisal habits so that they can become less biased. . . ."[13] Dr. Judith Beck, an expert on cognitive therapy, said that thoughts determine behavior, and cognitive therapy helps individuals pinpoint thoughts that lead to destructive or undesirable behavior.[14]

HOW YOU CAN USE COGNITIVE RESTRUCTURING TO ERADICATE YOUR NEGATIVE BELIEFS ABOUT AFRICAN AMERICAN STUDENTS

You can use cognitive restructuring to increase your efficacy with African American students simply by using the following steps, which are based on the works of Dombeck and Wells-Moran, as well as Beck. Although these authors used cognitive therapy to help individuals quit smoking or lose weight, rather than deal with mental baggage about African Americans, I believe that the strategies they recommend can also be beneficial to individuals who are attempting to work on other issues. As Dombeck and Wells-Moran stated, "Cognitive restructuring is the best studied and best understood technique for changing thoughts...."[15] Therefore, for the next 21 days, please use the following strategies, and record your efforts in a journal. I'm asking you to use the strategies for 21 consecutive days because I once heard that it takes *at least* 21 days to break a bad habit!

EXERCISE 2G: 21 DAYS OF COGNITIVE RESTRUCTURING

1. *Monitor yourself.* Dombeck and Wells-Moran define this type of self-monitoring as "learning to become more aware" of how you think in order to "become more conscious of your automatic thoughts...."[16] These authors emphasize that it is important to *record* your thoughts "shortly after some event has occurred that causes you to feel bad."[17] However, because educators often engage in destructive behaviors toward African American students without apparently feeling bad about their actions, I recommend that for the next 21 days, you record as many of your thoughts and actions that deal with African American students and African American adults as often as possible.

2. *Try to become aware of negative thoughts about African Americans when they occur.* Dombeck and Wells-Moran said that certain common ways of thinking, such as overgeneralizing, paying selective attention to events, ignoring or minimizing positive behaviors, and "all-or-nothing" thinking, are among the types of thoughts that you should try to become aware of.[18]

3. *Criticize and critique negative thoughts about African Americans when they occur.* This important strategy will require you to determine if your negative thoughts are based on fact or on your mental baggage or history of viewing African American students stereotypically. According to Dombeck and Wells-Moran, "When you really examine

your judgments carefully, looking for evidence to support them, you find that there is none. You are then in a position to form a new, more accurate appraisal."[19]

4. *At the end of 21 days, reread your entire journal, and write a summary of what it reveals about your beliefs, actions, progress, and areas on which you still need to work.*

5. *Continue to use the strategies and record your thoughts as part of your ongoing professional development.* (I'll say more about this in Chapter 3 and in the conclusion of this book.)

GROUP ACTIVITY FOR PROFESSIONAL DEVELOPMENT AND COURSE WORK

1. In a small group setting (no more than three or four individuals per group), share one or more excerpts from your journal with the group.

2. Ask for suggestions from the group about any area of difficulty that you are experiencing.

3. Brainstorm reasons why each group member should continue to do the cognitive restructuring work.

4. Make a commitment to encourage each other by telephone or e-mail at least once per week to continue to do the cognitive restructuring work.

3

"You Can't Help but Talk About Race"

Examining Your Beliefs
About Racism and Racial Problems

D o you ever get tired of hearing about racial issues? I know that I do. Like many Americans, I wish that we could all get along and live as "one big, happy American family." Unfortunately, this isn't the case. In fact, in the past year, as a result of President Barack Obama's unprecedented victory as the first black president of the United States, the media have devoted a considerable amount of attention to racial issues. Several years ago, *The New York Times* and CBS conducted a poll and concluded that Americans continue to be "sharply divided by race."[1] Last year, CNN aired *Black in America*, an in-depth look at the experiences of African Americans, which included whites' views about blacks. After that, a controversy erupted on the television talk show *The View* when co-hosts Elisabeth Hasselbeck and Whoopi Goldberg got into an argument over the "N word." The bottom line is that race continues to be a hot topic in this country, and related discussions can lead to misunderstandings, fear, and further racial polarization.

During the professional development workshops that I conduct, and presentations that I give throughout the nation, I find that many educators are just as uncomfortable as most other Americans when it comes to having honest and forthright conversations about race—at least in public settings. In fact, numerous teachers have told me that they don't even feel comfortable discussing racial issues in their classrooms. However, many of these same educators appear to desperately want to learn more about how to increase their efficacy with African American students. Unfortunately, fear of sounding racist, fear of being verbally attacked, or fear of sounding "stupid" are barriers that prevent countless educators from making progress in this area. Therefore, in this chapter, we'll look specifically at racism and racial issues. I'll answer three questions: (1) What is racism? (2) Why is racism such a big deal to African Americans? and (3) Why should educators care about racism? I will also ask you to continue with the mindset work that you began in the previous chapter and to go a step further by reading stories and research about racism and completing related exercises. Before we continue, please complete the following exercise.

EXERCISE 3A: YOUR THOUGHTS ABOUT RACISM AND RACIAL PROBLEMS

1. What is your definition of racism?

_____

_____

2. Have you ever experienced racism?

_____

_____

If so, explain when and where the incident(s) occurred, who was involved, and how you were affected.

_____

_____

3. In your opinion, are race relations in the United States better than they were when you were growing up, about the same as they were when you were growing up, or worse than they were when you were growing up? Please explain your answer.

_____

_____

4. How often do you think about racism and racial problems?

_____

_____

5. In your opinion, what are the main causes of racial problems in the United States?

_____

_____

6. Explain why you do or do not believe that racism will be eradicated during your lifetime.

_____

_____

★　★　★　★　★

I hope that you responded to the previous exercise as honestly and as courageously as possible. Later in this chapter, you'll be able to compare your responses to the responses of educators who addressed several of the same questions and statements during workshops that I conducted. But first, let's start with the basics by looking at the definitions of three terms that might be confusing to you: *racial prejudice*, *discrimination*, and *racism*.

WHAT IS RACISM?

According to Dr. Derald Wing Sue, an author and nationally known racism expert, racism, racial prejudice, and discrimination are three different problems. A person who is guilty of racial prejudice uses generalizations and stereotypes as an excuse to harbor negative views or biases about an entire racial group. A person who treats individuals or groups differently because of his or her racial prejudice engages in racial discrimination. Racism consists of the structures and widespread practices and policies that keep certain racial groups at a lower level or status in society.[2] Although any individual—including African Americans—can be guilty of being prejudiced or engaging in discriminatory behavior, only whites can be racist, according to Sue, because in the United States, whites are the only group that has the power to carry out discriminatory practices on a *widespread* level.[3]

Dr. Barbara Trepagnier, a professor, author, and white expert on racism, said that people of color often have a different definition of racism than whites. Furthermore, she said that racism can be covert, "unintended," and "silent." The silent and unintended forms of racism are two of the main reasons that racism continues to be common in the United States—because many whites are either in denial or ignorant about the ways in which they perpetuate racism.[4]

According to experts, one of the main reasons that many whites are in denial and are reluctant to admit that they harbor racial prejudice that prompts them to engage in racist behaviors is because, as a privileged group, whites have actually benefitted from racism. Just by nature of being born with "white" skin, most whites receive opportunities and privileges that blacks and other groups don't have. For example, Sue identified 20 privileges that whites automatically have that people of color do not. This white privilege is most evident in what Sue refers to as the Standard Operating Procedures (SOPS) in America. These SOPS have created institutional racism in most organizations, including banking, housing, schools, health care, employment, law enforcement, the media, and the courts, and they are designed to favor whites.[5]

WHY IS RACISM SUCH A BIG DEAL TO AFRICAN AMERICANS?

Although we now have a black U.S. president, racism still exists in nearly every sector of society. In the February 2009 issue of *Ebony* magazine, Linda Johnson Rice, the Chairman and CEO of Johnson Publishing Company, wrote:

> While Obama's election serves as a welcome triumph against racism, that triumph in no way signals racism's elimination. Believe it or not, racism will continue to be quite evident in the way African Americans are treated by the police, the courts, and the corrections system. The same is true when it comes to employment, housing, health care, and a number of other necessities that are influenced by racism that disproportionately impact the lives of Black Americans—every day.[6]

In other words, racism continues to be a big deal to many African Americans because history and research have repeatedly shown that black people are more likely than other groups to be subjected to racism at every level of society. In fact, a recent poll indicated that 51% of the blacks who participated said that they had been the victims of racial discrimination, while only 26% of whites said they had.[7] The poll results also showed the following:

- Most Americans consider racism to be a problem in the United States.
- Blacks are more than twice as likely to call racism a "very serious" problem in the United States as whites.
- Almost half of blacks and whites know someone who is racist.
- Most people say that they themselves aren't racist.[8]

The prevalence of racism in the lives of many African Americans has also been linked to health problems. Noted author bell hooks said that the fear of racism causes constant anxiety for many black people.[9] African American therapist Nancy Boyd-Franklin has treated African Americans for racism-related psychological problems.[10] Other researchers have found that there is a link between racism and depression in African Americans.[11] In other words, as renowned African American psychiatrist Dr. Alvin Poussaint and Dr. Boyd-Franklin concluded, racism can destroy African Americans mentally and physically.[12] These are some of the main reasons that racism continues to be a big deal to black people.

WHY SHOULD EDUCATORS CARE ABOUT RACISM?

There are several reasons why you, as an educator, should be concerned about racism. First, racism at school has harmed and continues to harm countless K–12 students. Second, institutional racism continues to exist in schools through policies and common practices that are harmful to African Americans and other students from historically marginalized backgrounds. In every study that I have conducted involving African American youth, a substantial percentage of the youth said that they experienced racism at school from teachers, administrators, staff, and other students. In addition, in *What African American Parents Want Educators to Know,* many parents and guardians said that their children were subjected to racism at school.[13] In a highly publicized study, researchers found that "twenty-three percent more Black youth than Whites believe that Black youth receive a poorer education on average than do White youth" and only 11% of black youth believe "that it is *very likely* that racism will be eliminated during their lifetime."[14]

Some educators are also aware of the effects of racism in schools. In the Mindset Study that I conducted, for example, 25% of the educators in Texas and nearly half of the preservice teachers in California who completed the questionnaire said that racism is the main reason why many African American K–12 students do not do as well as they could academically (see Appendix E).

In the Mindset Study, the educators and preservice teachers were also asked to respond to the statement, "In my opinion, most teachers treat and view most African American K–12 students in the same ways that they treat and view most non-Black students." The overwhelming majority of respondents in each subgroup (preservice teachers, teachers, administrators, whites, nonwhites, African Americans, males, and females) disagreed that most teachers treat and view black K–12 students in the same ways as most nonblack students. Nonwhites (84%) (especially blacks, 98%) and preservice teachers (82%) were more likely than other subgroups to disagree with this statement. However, 70% or more of females, teachers, administrators, and whites, and nearly 70% of the males made it clear that African American students are treated differently (see Appendix E).

Another reason that educators should be concerned about racism is because many of their colleagues apparently are. For example, during workshops that I conducted in 2007 and 2008, I asked three groups of educators to complete a questionnaire called "Thoughts About Racism and Racial Problems." One group worked at a private college preparatory high school in Los Angeles County. Another group worked in a California desert community, and the third group worked in Minnesota. (See Appendix H for demographic information about the respondents.) A total of 203 educators, the majority of whom were white, female K–12 teachers, completed the questionnaire. When asked how often they think about racism and racial problems, nearly 60% said that they think about these issues often. (See Appendix I for more information about the "Thoughts About Racism and Racial Problems" questionnaire.) When you responded to this question for Exercise 3A, how did you respond?

Another reason that educators should be concerned about racism is because many educators believe that our country has not made much progress in this area, and many appear to be hopeless about our nation's future in terms of race relations. For example, nearly half of the workshop participants who responded to the "Thoughts About Racism and Racial Problems" questionnaire said that race relations are basically the same as they were when they were growing up, and 16% said that they are worse. What did you say when you answered this question for Exercise 3A? The most disturbing finding was that more than 80% of the respondents said that they don't believe that racism will end in their lifetime. Did you say the same thing when you responded to this question for Exercise 3A, or were you more optimistic?

Like yourself, the workshop participants were also asked "In your opinion, what are the main causes of racial problems in the United States?" The most frequently cited answers were

- old ideas/beliefs/stereotypes/biases (35%),
- inequality/poverty/segregation/isolation (35%),
- ignorance (27%),
- education/lack of education (23%),
- fear (18%),
- lack of interracial experiences and interactions (18%),
- institutional racism (17%),
- misunderstandings (17%),
- media and racial profiling (16%),
- history (15%),
- adults/parents (14%), and
- sense of entitlement/superiority/white supremacy (13%).

EXERCISE 3B: COMPARE AND CONTRAST

1. How is the above list similar to or different from your own responses to this question (from Exercise 3A)?

_____

_____

2. What can you learn from the workshop participants' responses to the "Thoughts About Racism and Racial Problems" questionnaire?

_____

_____

3. What can you learn from your own responses to the questionnaire?

_____

_____

On the above list, "old ideas/beliefs/stereotypes/biases" and "ignorance" were two of the most frequently cited responses. In the previous chapter, I asked you to spend some time examining your beliefs and any stereotypes that you might have about African Americans, and I'll continue to ask you to do so as you read this book. Examining our beliefs is extremely important because when we aren't aware of the negative beliefs that we harbor about students and parents, we can knowingly or unknowingly engage in behaviors and create classroom policies that may be viewed as racist. In other words, if we are ignorant about our mindsets and beliefs, we can actually harm students. The following story is one of the best examples of this that I know. One of my African American doctoral students shared it in class one night. Her story is so powerful that I asked her for permission to use it in this book. She not only said "yes," but she also permitted me to interview her and later sent me a detailed explanation of the story that you are about to read. In fact, she said, "I really hope telling the story will help teachers realize their impact." To protect her identity, I will refer to her as "Amina."

AMINA'S STORY: "I DIDN'T GET THAT IT WAS JUST BECAUSE I WAS BLACK."

Amina grew up in a two-parent, middle-class family. Like Nathan, in the previous chapter, her parents believed so strongly in the value of a good education that they placed her in a private elementary school. Like Nathan, she also excelled academically because her parents expected this of her. Unlike Nathan, at the private elementary school that she attended, Amina had teachers who had high expectations of her. Therefore, she loved school and had very positive school-related experiences. However, for some reason that she didn't explain to me, when Amina was in the middle of third grade, her parents enrolled her in a public school for the first time. This marked the beginning of one of the most stressful and confusing periods of her childhood.

Although Amina didn't say much about the few months that she spent in a third-grade public school classroom, she did speak extensively about fourth grade. "The fourth grade was when I had the teacher who went berserk, and I didn't get that it was just because I was black," she told me. "I didn't get it at first." Amina, who was the only African American child in her class, had a white female teacher whose age was difficult for her to determine. "She could have been 20," Amina said, "but she seemed older, like 40." But it wasn't the teacher's age that was problematic; it was her beliefs about African American students. These beliefs caused the teacher to engage in both covert and overt racist behaviors. Consequently, fourth grade turned out to be the worst year of Amina's entire K–12 education. According to Amina:

> In school, I was often charged with cheating. This was another form of racism I so often encountered. At my old private school, they demanded excellence. At my new public school, I was being punished for it. In fourth grade, I never misspelled a word on our weekly spelling quizzes. I had perfect spelling. She [the teacher] could not believe it. The highest [scoring student] got free stuff: free lunch or coupons, stickers, stars, that type of thing. I would always get it.
>
> The teacher would move my seat before quizzes to ensure I was not cheating. She went as far as to have me sit at a side table with my paper and pencil [so that I could] complete the quiz under her watchful eye.
>
> She also stopped legibly writing my "A+" grade on my quizzes. When I asked for an explanation, she said if I looked carefully, I would find the "A+" grade. She also said that since I wrote very small, my grade would be small. She would write my "A+" very small, in awkward places, and upside down in those awkward places. I would search and search and search. Sometimes, I found it in the very upper corner in micro script or even upside down or on the back of the paper.
>
> Many of the things she taught us about grammar and orthography, I already knew because I read incessantly, and my father was also teaching me at home. I always raised my hand to answer

the questions she posed to the class, but she never called on me after the first couple of months. I had more than double the amount of gold stars for performance on the wall as all the other students, and she still refused to name me "Student of the Month." At one point, she started reviewing the exam questions for students while making me sit outside (within her view) on the bench.

In spite of the teacher's blatant differential treatment toward her, Amina continued to excel academically, but the effects were surfacing outside of the classroom. "I didn't get it at first," Amina explained. "I just knew she hated me." Unfortunately, it wasn't just the teacher who mistreated Amina. Because teachers set the tone for how students behave in class, the teacher knowingly or unknowingly gave Amina's white classmates permission to mistreat her. "I was being told by my peers to 'Go back to Africa,' being called 'African booty scratcher,' 'tar baby,' 'Aunt Jemima,' and of course, 'Nigger!'" she said. Eventually, Amina's behavior started to change. She explained:

> That's the year that I started picking my hair out from anxiety. My oppositional encounters with this teacher and some of my peers caused me to start pulling my hair [out] from the roots, sucking my left thumb, and wetting the bed. This was the year I visited a psychologist for the first time for anxiety.
>
> My mom did sit in that class once because my behavior had changed so much, and I was getting in trouble at school. The teacher was nice to my mom but said "Something's not right with [your daughter]." But she would never do [the mean things] when my mom was there. I know my mom. Had [the teacher] done any of those things when my mom was there, then there would've been a confrontation.

Because being well behaved and docile had only caused heartbreak for her, Amina became less passive and began to speak up. To her surprise, the teacher couldn't handle this. "When I complained that it was not fair to punish me for being a good student, she left class one day. [She was] upset at me and never returned." However, at the time, Amina didn't realize that her teacher's absence had allegedly been prompted by her complaints. Later, she heard it from one of the substitute teachers. According to Amina:

> We had substitute teachers the rest of that year, the first of whom did not hesitate to inform me that I was responsible for the original teacher's breakdown because I was a difficult student. She told me that the teacher "couldn't take it anymore" because of what I was doing to her. The sub already knew who I was.

Evidently, the other substitute teachers who came later did so also, and Amina's situation didn't improve much while they were in charge. She explained:

> At the end of that year, the last substitute granted me the "Most Improved Student" award. When I questioned it, I was informed that the record book showed I had failed to turn in many assignments at the beginning of the year. My heart was broken and I was angry, realizing that my original teacher had posted my gold stars on the classroom wall, but failed to officially record much of the work I submitted to her. In fourth grade, I learned that no one likes a know-it-all, especially when she is black.

Although Amina learned this painful lesson in fourth grade, she continued to excel academically in fifth grade. After all, this is what her parents and private school teachers had groomed her to do. Unfortunately, like her fourth-grade teacher, her fifth-grade teacher wasn't pleased to have a high-achieving African American child in his class either. However, this teacher engaged mostly in covert, rather than overt, racist behaviors. According to Amina:

> In fifth grade, it all continued with the new teacher. I far surpassed the other students, finished my work before lunch recess, completed my homework in class, and won all the state capital contests he held each week. Although he practiced more covert racism, I actually liked him a little because I never felt seriously threatened by him.
>
> As an adult [now], I sincerely believe he wanted to treat me fairly and liked having a bright student, but he just could not overcome his racist beliefs. Moreover, my performance in his class continued to challenge those beliefs. He never called me a cheater, but he told me he might think about granting me the "Student of the Month" award at the end of the year. I did not like it, and I was upset, so I childishly began blurting out all the answers to his questions, once I realized he would only call on me when no one else was able to answer.
>
> He sent me to the office for defiance many times. So in April of that school year, I became so angry that I orchestrated an unsuccessful fifth-grade ditch day in protest. Only 10 of my friends and acquaintances ditched school with me that day, but it was successful in that it got me moved from that classroom into a sixth-grade classroom as a fifth-grade visitor.
>
> When the sixth-grade teacher saw that I was able to do the same work as her students, she began teaching me as if I were a sixth-grade student. At the end of the year, I was given the choice

to go on to sixth grade in September or be promoted to seventh grade. I was 10 years old, and afraid of junior high, but I was so tired of my elementary school. My parents let me decide to go on to the seventh grade.

The negative experiences that Amina had with public elementary school teachers and some of her classmates had a long-term effect on her. For awhile, she gave up on the education system. After all, why wouldn't she, given the fact that she had been punished by teachers for being a high achiever? In fact, Amina said, "I didn't know that I *wasn't* supposed to be smart," until she attended public school! During one difficult period, she became an underachieving discipline problem who was on a downward path of academic, and possibly even lifelong, failure. However, I am extremely happy to report that this story has a very happy ending. Amina eventually recaptured her belief in the importance of a good education and once again became the high achiever that she had always been. After graduating with honors from a prestigious private university, she wrote a book and enrolled in a doctoral studies program. Today, after earning numerous awards and honors, she is happily married and close to earning her doctorate.

EXERCISE 3C: LEARNING FROM AMINA'S STORY

1. Why did Amina believe that her fourth- and fifth-grade teachers were racist? Explain why you agree or disagree with her conclusions about them.

_____

_____

2. In what ways are you similar to and different from Amina's fourth-grade teacher?

_____

_____

3. In what ways are you similar to and different from her fifth-grade teacher?

_____

_____

4. Why would a teacher feel threatened by a high-achieving African American student?

_____

_____

5. Are you equally as comfortable working with high-achieving African American students as you are with average and low-achieving African American students? Why or why not?

_____

_____

6. Explain why you believe that the fourth-grade teacher was or was not responsible for the way that Amina's white classmates treated her.

_____

_____

7. What are the three main lessons that you learned from Amina's story?

_____

_____

8. Have you ever witnessed a student being subjected to racism at school? If so, how did you react?

_____

_____

9. Have you ever knowingly or unknowingly subjected a student to racism?

_____

_____

10. Explain why you would or wouldn't get involved if a student complained to you that a teacher or student was discriminating against him or her because of the student's race.

_____

_____

11. Explain what you would do if a colleague made racist statements to you about one or more students, a parent, or even about another colleague.

_____

_____

12. What racist beliefs do you harbor against students from racial backgrounds that are different from your own?

_____

_____

MOVING FORWARD

I hope that one of the lessons you learned from Amina's story is how dangerous it is for us to have unexamined beliefs about our students, particularly our African American students. Educators who are in denial or who are unaware that they harbor racial prejudice can knowingly or unknowingly engage in behaviors that can have far-reaching consequences. Although Amina's story had a happy ending, in many cases, African American K–12 students never recover from the racism that they experience at school from adults and other students, and many adults who become societal failures do so because of the negative messages that they internalized about themselves from people at school.

Another message that I hope you inferred from Amina's story is that teachers can create a hostile classroom environment by giving students permission to act out racial prejudices. As I said earlier in this chapter, many educators have told me that when racial conflicts arise in their classrooms, they don't know how to address them and many end up ignoring them. No teacher should permit other students to engage in or use any type of offensive behavior or language in class, including profanity, sexist language, or racist language.

A third lesson that I hope you learned from this story is that if racism is going to be eradicated in our lifetimes, and if all students are going to be able to attend school and sit in classrooms where they are treated fairly and humanely by educators and classmates, then each individual will have to play a role in destroying racism—the big fat stinky elephant that continues to sit right in America's living room and in classrooms throughout the nation.

Without a doubt, educators can and must play a crucial role in helping the United States move forward in terms of race relations. The question is how? Please answer this question by completing the following exercise.

EXERCISE 3D: SEARCHING FOR SOLUTIONS

1. In your opinion, what will it take for racism and racial problems to be eradicated in the United States?

_____

_____

2. What role can you play in eradicating racism at your school site?

_____

_____

3. How can you decrease the likelihood that your African American students will believe that you are a racist?

_____

_____

Before I share my own recommendations about the questions that you just answered, I want to return to the "Thoughts About Racism and Racial Problems" questionnaire that 203 workshop participants in California and Minnesota completed (see Appendix I). Like you, these educators were asked, "In your opinion, what will it take for racism and racial problems to be eradicated in the United States?" Look at the following list of the seven most frequently cited responses, and compare and contrast your own recommendations to the list.

- Better education (45%)
- More opportunities/eliminate economic barriers (29%)
- More dialogue/greater awareness (24%)
- Cross-cultural/cross-racial interactions (21%)
- Better leadership (17%)
- Take personal responsibility (16%)
- Improve school system (12%)
- Avoid stereotyping/sensationalism (9%)

Six of the categories of responses consist of recommendations that educators can use to eliminate racism: better education, more dialogue/greater awareness, cross cultural/cross-racial interactions, better leadership, take personal responsibility, and improve schools. As an educator, here are some ways that you can make a difference:

- Continue to educate yourself and your students about racism, racial prejudice, and discrimination.
- Use the curriculum to create opportunities for students to have discussions and, thereby, greater awareness about racial issues.
- Through group work and other collaborative exercises, encourage students from different racial backgrounds to work together.
- Groom students to become leaders by having them tackle societal problems such as racism through research projects, writing assignments, and group work.
- Encourage students to make a choice to take personal responsibility for not making racist remarks and choosing not to discriminate against people from a different racial background.

Obviously, before you can do this important work with your students, you must also be willing to do these things on a personal level. For example, are you willing to take personal responsibility for your own actions in terms of how you treat African American students? Are you willing to have ongoing discussions about racial issues with your colleagues from different racial backgrounds in order to better educate yourself and improve your cross-racial relations? Are you willing to take a leadership role at your school in order to raise awareness about racial issues and help colleagues brainstorm solutions?

The 69 educators at a private college preparatory high school and a public school in California who completed the "Searching for Solutions" questionnaire also had a chance to explain how educators can change any negative mindsets and stereotypes that they have about African American students (see Appendix G). The following list contains the five most frequently cited categories of responses that they gave:

- Education/awareness/inservices for teachers (57%)
- Face biases/identify stereotypes/engage in introspection (41%)
- Make a personal choice/commit to change (23%)
- Use the community, students, and parents as resources (16%)
- Improve teacher behavior and practices (15%)

As you can see, their list was similar to the responses of the educators who completed the "Thoughts About Racism and Racial Problems" questionnaire. Respondents who completed the questionnaires made it clear that racial problems will only be solved when we do a better job of educating ourselves and others, when we are willing to face our personal biases, when we are willing to take personal responsibility, and when we are willing to have dialogues and discussions with people from racial backgrounds that are different from our own. With this in mind, I want to encourage you to continue to do the cognitive restructuring work that I asked you to begin doing at the end of Chapter 2. The following list contains the main strategies that I described at the end of Chapter 2, and I've added additional suggestions to help you move forward with your efforts to become a more effective educator of African American students.

COGNITIVE RESTRUCTURING CONTINUED

1. *Continue to monitor yourself.* For the next 21 days, record as many of your thoughts and actions that deal with African American students and African American adults as often as possible.

2. *Try to become aware of negative thoughts that you have about African American students and their parents when they occur.*

3. *Criticize and critique negative thoughts when they occur.*

4. *At the end of the second 21-day period, reread your entire journal, and write a summary of what it reveals about your beliefs, actions, progress, and areas on which you still need to work.*

5. *Continue to use the strategies and record your thoughts as often as possible.*

6. Read *Through Ebony Eyes: What Teachers Need to Know but Are Afraid to Ask About African American Students.* When you finish reading the book, create a racism unit that you can actually use with your students, and set a timeline for actually teaching this unit so that it won't just collect dust somewhere.

7. *Leave your comfort zone by making a choice to interact more with your African American colleagues.* You can ask one or more of them to recommend a good book for you to read that can help you to better understand African American culture, students, parents, and so on. You can invite one or more of your African American colleagues to lunch and start a dialogue, or even an ongoing discussion group, about best teaching practices for African American students.

8. *Read the following books and record your thoughts and the lessons that you learn in your journal:*

   • *White Teachers/Diverse Classrooms,* by Julie Landsman and Chance Lewis
   • *Growing Up White: A Veteran Teacher Reflects on Racism,* by Julie Landsman
   • *Courageous Conversations About Race: A Field Guide for Achieving Equity in Schools,* by Glenn Singleton and Curtis Linton
   • *It's the Little Things: Everyday Interactions That Anger, Annoy, and Divide the Races,* by Lena Williams
   • *Silent Racism: How Well-Meaning White People Perpetuate the Racial Divide,* by Barbara Trepagnier
   • *Overcoming Our Racism: The Journey to Liberation,* by Derald Wing Sue
   • *The Dreamkeepers: Successful Teachers of African American Children,* by Gloria Ladson Billings
   • *Up Where We Belong: Helping African American and Latino Students Rise in School and in Life,* by Gail L. Thompson

EXERCISE 3E: REFLECTING ON QUOTES ABOUT RACISM

In order to remind you of how important it is for you to be brave and honest in facing any racial baggage that you are carrying, and also to help your students deal with their own racial baggage, I conclude this chapter with quotes from some of the educators who have attended workshops and presentations that I have given. After you read the quotes, I'll ask you to write a response.

"You can't help but talk about race." (An African American middle school principal)

1. Explain why you agree or disagree with this statement.

_____

_____

"Everyone sees the world differently and treats people accordingly. In order to rectify these differences we must gain an understanding of those we will be working with and be accepting. Ignorance is not a valid excuse and shame on teachers who succumb to this. Social consciousness and awareness are among the leading tools to counteract and eliminate ignorance." (First-year male teacher)

2. Explain why you agree or disagree with this statement.

_____

_____

"I have seen many teachers throughout my training that are racist toward their African American students through the hidden curriculum. It is unfair for the child and this should be pointed out to those teachers that unconsciously do it, and especially to those who intentionally do it." (First-year Latina elementary school teacher)

3. Explain why you agree or disagree with this statement.

_____

_____

"I will say that no teacher, in my mind, would intentionally be biased or treat students differently. But we sometimes unknowingly do these things. I agree that teachers must take the extra step to educate themselves about culture and to make the effort to give each child equal opportunities to get a great education. We will have to take additional steps for those children who have already been left behind. We, as teachers, have to embrace and respect students' primary culture and language while teaching them to speak, write, and communicate well in Standard English." (First-year Filipina teacher)

4. Explain why you agree or disagree with this statement.

_____

_____

5. Based on what you've learned in this chapter, what steps are you willing to take to eliminate any racial baggage that you have that could impede your progress with African American students?

_____

_____

★   ★   ★   ★   ★

GROUP ACTIVITY FOR PROFESSIONAL DEVELOPMENT AND COURSE WORK

Each group member can read one of the recommended texts in this chapter and share the main ideas with the rest of the group during a "book talk."

4

"To Be Honest, I Can't Stand His Mama"

Facing Your Personal Issues
About the Parents of African American Students

One day, during the time that I was writing this book, I watched an interesting episode of Tyra Banks's television show. On this particular episode, which focused on stereotypes and racism, Tyra interviewed several adults and children. One group of interviewees consisted of a white family—a mother, father, and their two children. Although the children were only in elementary school, the parents had already programmed them to believe negative stereotypes about African Americans and Jews, and the parents made many blatantly racist remarks on the show. I wasn't surprised by any of these white supremacists' racist comments. In fact, they sounded so ignorant and backwards that I didn't even bother to get upset over their remarks. But another segment of the show made a different impact on me.

The other segment featured an elementary school teacher and her racially diverse students. The teacher showed the students photos of several individuals and asked questions such as, "Which one would make the best president?" "Which person is smartest?" "Which person is the best athlete?" and so on. Two things quickly became very clear from the children's responses: First, all of the children who replied based their remarks on stereotypes. Second, even though they were only in elementary school, all of the children who spoke believed that black people are less intelligent than nonblacks. Sadly, the black children in the group seemed to believe the negative stereotypes about blacks just as much as their nonblack classmates did.

This segment of the show didn't shock me, but it did make me sad, for it goes to show how effective the antiblack propaganda "machine" that has existed in the United States for centuries has been in brainwashing society, even young children, about African Americans. For example, one of the little white boys in the class said that black people don't work as hard as other groups and that black children miss a lot of school. This child was merely saying what countless adults believe about African Americans. Therefore, it's no surprise that stereotypes about African American parents, the main topic of this chapter, are just as common.

A BRIEF HISTORY LESSON

Most Americans don't believe that African American parents are good parents, and most don't believe that we care about our children's education. What these individuals—and even many black educators—don't know is that education has *always* been highly valued by black people, starting in Africa. For example, in *African Americans: Voices of Triumph: Leadership*, the editors described many outstanding African American leaders, scientists, businessmen, businesswomen, educators, preachers, and politicians. However, they made it clear that long before the first Africans came to America, there were exemplary Africans on the continent of Africa who excelled in all of these areas. The editors referred to "Africa's rich history," to Africa as "the cradle of civilization," and wrote of "the thousands of extraordinary men and women" that Africa produced. They also refuted the horrible stereotypes and lies that Europeans have spread about Africa throughout the centuries.[1] In another book, *Hard Road to Freedom: The Story of African America,* authors James Oliver Horton and Lois E. Horton described several great African civilizations and the rich legacy that Africa passed on to the world. For instance, in Timbuktu, an ancient African city, there were 180 schools, and people traveled from around the world to visit the university that was located there.[2]

The value that black people have always placed on education has also been written about by other historians, particularly experts on the experiences of African Americans during slavery and after it ended in the United States. During the slavery era, although slaves and free blacks were desperate to learn to read and write, the United States government allowed many laws to be created that made it difficult for blacks to become literate.[3] In spite of the strong opposition from racist whites, African Americans were determined to get an education for themselves and their children. Many historians, including African American scholars such as Dr. W. E. B. Du Bois, Dr. James Anderson, Dr. Charles Johnson, and Dr. John Hope Franklin wrote about the enthusiasm with which the former slaves pursued education.[4] In fact, Du Bois wrote, "The eagerness to learn among American Negroes was exceptional. . . ."[5]

This hard work and determination paid off because, even though most blacks were illiterate when the Civil War ended, by 1909, nearly 4,000 blacks had earned college degrees,[6] and by 1910, 70% of African Americans could read and write.[7] Since then, African Americans have continued to fight for equal educational opportunities on many fronts: at the K–12 school level, the college level, and through the courts. Today, that struggle continues.

THE PLIGHT OF THE PARENTS OF AFRICAN AMERICAN K–12 STUDENTS

One of the easiest ways for educators to see examples of this struggle is to place themselves in the shoes of the parents of African American K–12 students. I often receive e-mails and telephone calls from some of these desperate parents, and during my workshops and presentations, I often hear educators complaining about the parents of African American students. It is apparent to me that there are *major* misunderstandings on both sides. Many black parents believe that educators treat their children unfairly, and many educators believe that most African American parents don't care about their children's education. Therefore, in the presentations that I give to church groups and other organizations that are predominated by African American parents, I try to help African American parents learn how to become more effective advocates for their children. Also, in my book *A Brighter Day: How Parents Can Help African American Youth,*[8] I described numerous strategies that parents can use to help their children be successful inside and outside of school. Conversely, when dealing with groups of educators, I try to help this audience better understand African American parents and their children.

In the remainder of this chapter, my goal is to help you better understand the parents of African American students. In the following sections, you'll read stories that two mothers of African American boys shared with me. I included these stories, related exercises, and research to help you improve your relations with African American parents and increase your efficacy with their children. The first story is based on an e-mail that I received, in 2005, from a white woman who contacted me after seeing me discuss one of my books on *Tony Brown's Journal*, a national public television show. This Baltimore mother's detailed e-mail described her experiences as the parent of two half-black children.

A WHITE MOTHER'S STORY: "YEAR AFTER YEAR OF INSANITY WORE HIM DOWN."

According to her e-mail, many years earlier, this woman had married an African American man. However, "The marriage was doomed from the beginning, since it was more about race and politics than about love." But her reasons for contacting me had little to do with her marriage. She wanted to talk about her children—particularly one of her son's experiences with the public school system. Although they were both biracial boys being reared by a white mother, her sons had very different school experiences. "One of them had a cardio-pulmonary arrest as an infant, which left him identified as 'handicapped,' rather than 'black,'" the mother stated. Shockingly, this label *protected* him from the fate of his brother—a boy who was merely labeled as "black."

The woman explained that she had been very involved in her children's education. She never missed a parent–teacher conference and was always receptive when teachers contacted her about her son—the boy who, unlike his brother, had merely been labeled as black. Nevertheless, the problems started almost from the very beginning of his K–12 education.

When her son was in first grade, his teacher said, "He's smart, but he isn't working up to his potential." In second grade, he was suspended from school for "indecent exposure" because he couldn't hold himself and urinated where he thought no one was around. By fourth grade, his teacher was encouraging his mother to consider putting him on Ritalin, a drug that is commonly prescribed for hyperactivity.

When he was in junior high school, his teacher told his mother, "He's smart, but he's acting increasingly bizarre." By this time, the boy had become so depressed "that he was eventually hospitalized for six months." In ninth grade, he was sent home for three days for refusing to stand for the Pledge of Allegiance. When he was in tenth grade, a teacher told her, "He's smart but he's in a drunken stupor all day." The following year, a school official said, "He's smart, but off the record, we don't have a program that suits him, so we recommend he drop out and get a GED." During what was supposed to be his senior year of high school, the woman's son participated in an outreach program that allowed him to take college courses instead of the traditional high school curriculum. But the mother was told:

> He's smart, and we can see he finished a year of college in lieu of his senior year according to the terms of the state's outreach program, but that program was intended for our "A" students, and frankly, we lost interest in your son and haven't kept his records up to date. But here's a diploma for him, since we don't have any choice but to give him one.

Later, when this mother thought about her son's school experiences and how "year after year of insanity wore him down," she realized that both she and the school system had been at fault. Regarding the school system's treatment of her son, she stated, "The school's performance was shameless." But she also blamed herself for her ignorance about racism and the realities that African Americans, including biracial youth, must deal with in a so-called democratic nation. In her e-mail to me, she said:

> I always assumed they were right. Therein was my son's downfall. I grew up in a world that made sense, an all white environment where if something bad happened to you, it was because you had messed up. It was years before I realized my son was not growing up in a world that made sense, but rather where he could be treated completely out of proportion to what he might have done. It was a horrible thing to watch, in comparison to my own privileged youth. . . .

At the time when she e-mailed me, even though her son was no longer a student in the K–12 public school system, this mother's pain over his experiences had spurred her to action. She wanted to expose the racism that many students routinely experience and her goal was "to continue to try to do my part to educate 'my people' about privilege and oppression and how those play out in institutional racism."

This white mother realized some important lessons about the K–12 education system, and she realized them at a time when it was too late for her to be a strong advocate for her child. What she realized was that institutional racism is extremely prevalent in the education system, and for the most part, black children are not treated as fairly or as humanely as non-black children are treated.

EXERCISE 4A: RESPONDING TO A WHITE MOTHER'S STORY

Please respond to each of the following questions/statements as honestly as possible.

1. What was your overall impression of this story?

   _____

   _____

2. What are the three most important messages that you learned from this story?

   _____

   _____

   _____

3. How can you use this story to become a better educator of African American and biracial students?

_____

_____

4. What new information did you learn about parent–educator relations from this story?

_____

_____

★   ★   ★   ★   ★

An African American parent shared the next story with me during a telephone conversation. This mother of three had moved from California to Texas several years ago. Unlike the large city where she and her family had previously resided, the small town that they moved to in Texas was predominantly white. To protect her identity, I refer to her as "Misha" as I describe a negative experience that one of her sons had at school.

MISHA'S STORY: "HE DIDN'T WANT TO COME BACK TO SCHOOL."

Shortly after she moved her family to Texas, one of Misha's sons started having problems at his new elementary school. One day, the little third grader raised his hand and asked his teacher, a white woman, if he could go to the restroom. Although he was "a model student and not a discipline problem," according to Misha, "the teacher said, 'No.'"

Soon, Misha's son began to squirm in his seat, and yet according to his mother, "She wouldn't let my baby go to the bathroom." Later that day, Misha got a call from the school "saying my baby had peed on himself. He had never had an accident. He was never a discipline problem. He might finish his work early and want to get out of his seat to help somebody, but he was *never* a discipline problem." After urinating on himself at school, the child was traumatized. "My baby was too embarrassed to go back to school," his mother said.

Of course, Misha reacted as most parents in a similar situation would have reacted: She got angry! "I went up to that school," she told me, "and I set them straight. I said, 'Don't ever, ever [tell my child that he can't go to the restroom]. My son has been humiliated. His feelings are hurt. He didn't want to come back to school. He is eight years old.'"

EXERCISE 4B: RESPONDING TO MISHA'S STORY

Please respond to each of the following questions/statements as honestly as possible.

1. In your opinion, did Misha have a right to be angry about her son's experience at school? Why or why not?

   _____

   _____

2. In your opinion, was Misha justified in expressing her feelings to school officials? Why or why not?

   _____

   _____

3. If you were a parent in Misha's situation, how do you think you would have handled this situation?

   _____

   _____

4. In your opinion, what were the long-term consequences of the child's "accident"?

   _____

   _____

5. What are the main lessons that you learned from Misha's story?

   _____

   _____

6. What did Misha's story and "A White Mother's Story" teach you about parent–educator relations?

   _____

   _____

★ ★ ★ ★ ★

WHY SOME AFRICAN AMERICANS ARE AMBIVALENT ABOUT THE FORMAL EDUCATION SYSTEM

At the beginning of this chapter, I shared some of the research that shows that blacks have always valued education, even before the first African slaves were brought to America. This is true, but it's also true that some African Americans have ambivalent feelings about formal education. This stems from their own negative K–12 school experiences, and even their higher education experiences. Many African American parents, for example, received a substandard K–12 education; many went to college only to learn that, as a result of low teacher expectations at the schools they attended, they had weak academic skills and needed remediation. Also, during their own pursuit of education, many faced both subtle and overt racism from educators. Now, as parents who want to be advocates for their children, they often find themselves encountering some of the same problems that they themselves experienced. This can be extremely frustrating. To make matters worse, many educators remain in denial about the race-based differential experiences that African American students may have at school, and many automatically view African American parents as adversaries rather than allies. In the following exercise, you will get to share your views about this issue.

EXERCISE 4C: ALLY OR ADVERSARY?

Please respond to each of the following questions/statements as honestly as possible.

1. Do you tend to view African American parents as allies or adversaries? Please explain your answer.

   _____

   _____

2. In your opinion, are the parents of most African American K–12 students very concerned about their children's education? Please explain your answer.

   _____

   _____

3. How many unconcerned African American parents have you *personally* met, spoken to, or interacted with?

   _____

   _____

4. What gave you the impression that these parents were unconcerned about their children's education?

   _____

   _____

5. How many concerned African American parents have you *personally* met, spoken to, or interacted with?

_____

_____

6. What gave you the impression that these parents were concerned about their children's education?

_____

_____

7. Now, review your answers, and summarize what they reveal about your views of African American parents.

_____

_____

★ ★ ★ ★ ★

WHAT THE "MINDSET STUDY" REVEALED ABOUT HOW EDUCATORS VIEW AFRICAN AMERICAN PARENTS

I hope that you responded to the items in the previous exercise as honestly as possible because apparently, some educators have trouble being honest about their views—not only regarding African American students, but African American parents as well. The topic of "African American parents" surfaced twice in the "Mindset Study" that I conducted, and also in another study that I conducted, and the results underscore this point.

In the "Mindset Study," in response to the statement "In my opinion, most teachers believe that the parents or guardians of most African American K–12 students are very concerned about their education," the overwhelming majority of preservice teachers, teachers, administrators, whites, nonwhites, males, and females who completed the questionnaire said that most teachers do not believe that most African American parents are very concerned. In fact, more than 80% of administrators, whites, and African American respondents said this (see Appendix E). However, before I created the "Mindset Questionnaire," I asked the 71 teachers who attended a workshop that I conducted at a California elementary school to respond to the statement, "I honestly believe that most of my African American students have caring parents or guardians." Nearly all of the respondents said that they believed this (see Appendix C). In other words, it was easy for educators to say that *they* had a positive view of African American parents, but also easy for educators to say that *other educators* viewed them negatively.

The topic of African American parents also surfaced among the results of another "Mindset Questionnaire" item. When asked "What are the main reasons why many African American students do not do as well in school as they could?" the respondents were more likely to blame school factors than nonschool factors, a topic that I'll say more about in Chapter 5. However, nearly 30% blamed parents, and African American educators were more likely than any other group to do this (see Appendix E).

WHY SOME EDUCATORS MAY ASSUME THAT AFRICAN AMERICAN PARENTS DON'T CARE ABOUT THEIR CHILDREN'S EDUCATION

As I said previously, research shows that most African American parents care about their children's education, but many educators believe that they don't. There are several reasons why this confusion exists. In fact, I've written extensively about some of these reasons in two of my other books: *What African American Parents Want Educators to Know*[9] and *Up Where We Belong: Helping African American and Latino Students Rise in School and in Life.*[10] To better help you understand African American parents, I'll summarize some of these reasons.

First, as I've already stated, many African American parents had negative K–12 school experiences, and many also experienced racism during their pursuit of higher-education degrees. Therefore, some African American parents may be ambivalent about the U.S. education system. Educators may mistakenly equate this ambivalence with a lack of concern about their children's education.

Second, when parents fail to show up for "Open House" and "Back-to-School Night," many educators assume that it's because the parents aren't concerned about their children's education. However, many other factors—including the ones in the next sections of this chapter—may be the actual reasons that these parents don't attend these events. For example, a parent may not show up at these events because of transportation problems, childcare issues, or having to work late.

Third, some African American parents may limit their contact with educators and their time at the actual school site because they have been traumatized by recent negative experiences. For example, in 2007, after I gave a presentation in Atlanta, Georgia, an African American educator told me a related story. According to this wife, mother, and teacher, when her son became a fourth grader, she and her husband decided that her husband would take a more visible role in his education. Therefore, the father would now attend the parent–teacher conferences. But the first conference that he had with his son's teacher, a white woman, turned into a disaster.

According to the educator who relayed this story to me, "My husband is a big, ole teddy bear. He's soft spoken, easy-going, and laid back." On the day of his first conference with his son's fourth-grade teacher, he wore a business suit and was eager to meet her. The meeting between father and teacher began well, or so he thought. He and the teacher were in the middle of what the father thought was a simple conversation about his son's academic progress. But all of a sudden, a security guard rushed into the classroom. It turned out that "the teacher had pushed the panic button!" In other words, although the father had assumed that the meeting was going well, the teacher's concern over being alone in a room with a black man had caused her to become so anxious and fearful that she eventually pushed a hidden panic button that was within her reach.

A fourth reason why some African American parents may appear not to care about their children's education is that educators have given them mixed messages. I have repeatedly learned from my research and conversations with African American parents that although educators *say* they want African American parents to be more involved in their children's education, many educators don't really mean this. Through the actions of various educators, many African American parents have inferred that they are actually not wanted on campus. In fact, African American parents can find school sites to be unwelcoming and hostile places where they are treated rudely by staff, administrators, and teachers—and actually even subjected to harassment from security. Moreover, some African American parents who have tried to serve as advocates for their children have told me that their children have been retaliated against by teachers who gave them low grades in order to "punish" a vocal, involved, and proactive parent.

In late 2007, during a presentation that I gave at the "Racial Achievement Gap Summit" that was sponsored by State Superintendent Jack O'Connell in Sacramento, California, I addressed this point. I asked the audience, "If you are a black parent who has ever been mistreated or disrespected at a school for merely trying to be an advocate for your child, would you please stand?" Nearly every black educator in the audience stood. If black educators run into hostility from other educators when they try to help their children get a good education, how much more likely is the average black parent to receive mixed messages about parent involvement from educators and school staff?

Another reason that African American parents may not appear to be concerned about their children's education has to do with the level of academic support that a parent is able to give. Because countless parents attended substandard schools, and K–12 students today are required to have more advanced math skills at a younger age than previous generations did, it is very likely that many parents won't be able to help their children do some of the homework that is required—because of their own weak math skills. In addition, a black parent who was passed through the K–12 school system with poor reading skills might not know how to help her child develop good reading skills. For example, a former elementary school teacher recently told me that when she asked a parent to help her daughter with her homework, she learned that the mother couldn't read. The important point to remember is that just because a parent may not have the necessary skills to help a child in the ways that educators would like, that still doesn't mean that the parent isn't extremely concerned about his or her child's education. In fact, many parents whom educators label as being unconcerned may be engaging in activities in the privacy of their own homes that are designed to help children do well in school and that educators never see or hear about.[11]

There's also another reason: Some African American parents may appear not to care about their children's education because they are so overwhelmed by life that their children's education is actually low on their list of top priorities. During my presentations to educators, I often say that when I was growing up in a single-parent, low-income household, my mother cared about the education of all six of her children. However, because we were extremely poor—and were actually on welfare during part of my childhood—keeping a roof over our heads and keeping us fed and clothed were my mother's top priorities. Therefore, she didn't show up at school unless she absolutely had to. She didn't have time to sit down and help us with our homework or review our work. She did, however, make it clear to us that she expected us to earn decent grades, expected us to behave at school, and insisted that the older children help the younger ones with homework. She also modeled reading at home by constantly reading herself, and she permitted us to go to the "Bookmobile" to check out books. In other words, she cared about our education, but most of our teachers probably assumed that she didn't and looked down on her in much the same way that so many educators today disparage African American parents. The fact that many black parents are overwhelmed by the vicissitudes of life was also underscored by Dr. Reginald Clark in his excellent book *Family Life and School Achievement: Why Poor Black Children Succeed or Fail.*[12]

The last reason that I will address is that some African American parents may appear to be unconcerned about their children's education because they aren't aware of how they can support them academically. A parent who received an inferior K–12 education, who had poor parental role models, who dropped out of school, or who became a teen parent may not understand the role that he or she can play in helping a child do well in school. Nevertheless, this doesn't mean that the parent doesn't care about his or her child's academic welfare.

Regardless of what you may think of African American parents, I want you to keep two points in mind that I often share with educators who attend my workshops: (1) Children shouldn't be penalized for the homes from which they come. In other words, just as you didn't select your parents or decide the type of home environment in which you would grow up, neither did African American K–12 students. It is unfair for educators to shortchange children academically merely because they believe that the parents aren't measuring up to the ideal-parent standard that the educator has created. (2) Just as your students don't know what is going on in the privacy of your home, you can't assume that you know what is going on in their homes. The very parent that you may view as a failure may be working relentlessly to help his or her child do better at school. Just because you don't see the parent at the school events that you deem to be important, don't assume that it is evidence of a lack of caring on the parent's part.[13]

Now, I'm going to ask you to complete Exercise 4D as a way of reflecting on the information that you just read.

EXERCISE 4D: REFLECTING ON WHAT YOU HAVE LEARNED ABOUT AFRICAN AMERICAN PARENTS

Please respond to each of the following questions/statements as honestly as possible.

1. Summarize the main reasons that an African American parent may not appear to care about his or her child's education.

   _____

   _____

2. If you were the father who learned that your son's teacher had pushed a panic button during a parent–teacher conference, how do you think this would affect your desire to attend school functions, meet with teachers, and so on?

   _____

   _____

3. How can you use the information in the list of reasons why African American parents may not appear to be concerned about their children's education to improve your relations with African American parents?

   _____

   _____

WHY EDUCATORS MUST IMPROVE THEIR RELATIONS WITH AFRICAN AMERICAN PARENTS

For decades, researchers and policy makers have emphasized that parent involvement plays a crucial role in students' academic success. In fact, in February 2009, during one of his first public speeches after his inauguration, President Barack Obama spoke about the need for parents to be actively involved in their children's education. A lot of research shows that when parents are heavily involved in their children's education, the children tend to do better academically. However, parent involvement is beneficial not only to students, but to parents and educators as well. According to the National PTA, students whose parents are very involved in their education are more likely to earn good grades, have higher test scores, complete their homework, be well behaved at school, and attend college. Parents who are very involved in their children's education are more likely to use appropriate discipline strategies, to be more sensitive to children's developmental needs, to feel confident about their parenting skills, and to improve their own academic skills. Of course, educators benefit because they have the assistance of parents and they have students who are less likely to misbehave at school and who are more likely to complete their schoolwork and homework.[14]

HOW YOU CAN IMPROVE YOUR RELATIONS WITH AFRICAN AMERICAN PARENTS

Now that you've read about some of the reasons why African American parents may appear to be unconcerned about their children's education and how students, parents, and educators can benefit from parent involvement, the question that remains is "How can you improve your relations with African American parents in order to increase African American parent involvement?" Before I answer this question, I'd like you to complete the next exercise.

EXERCISE 4E: GETTING REAL WITH YOURSELF ABOUT AFRICAN AMERICAN PARENT INVOLVEMENT

Please respond to each of the following questions/statements as honestly as possible.

1. Do you *really want* to improve your relations with African American parents? Please explain your answer.

   _____

   _____

2. Are you willing to leave your comfort zone so that you can improve your relations with African American parents? Please explain your answer.

   _____

   _____

3. What, if any, questions, concerns, or fears do you have that might prevent you from improving your relations with African American parents?

_____

_____

4. Is there anyone at your school site, in the district office, or in the community where your students reside with whom you can discuss any fears, concerns, or questions that you have that might impede your progress with African American parents? If so, who is this person, and are you willing to contact him/her?

_____

_____

MOVING FORWARD

It is indeed possible for you to improve your relations with African American parents, and you've actually already taken the first step. That step is making a decision to do whatever is necessary to improve your relations with this misunderstood group of parents. If you answered "yes" to Question 1 in the previous exercise, then you are definitely ready. If you answered "no" or "I'm not sure," then you need to uncover the reasons why. That is why it is important to talk to other individuals who may be able to alleviate any fears or concerns that you have and answer related questions. The following strategies can help you move forward:

1. *Get rid of any negative mental baggage that you have about African American parents.* If you still have stereotypes about them or believe that they don't care about their children's education, your mindset may lead you to speak to them disparagingly or give them the impression that you are judging them negatively. This will make it difficult for you to be able to converse with African American parents in a professional and nonthreatening manner.

2. *Face your fears.* If you are terrified of African American parents because you believe that they are dangerous, violent, or aggressive, you will subconsciously erect barriers between them and yourself that will make it difficult for you to work effectively with them.

3. *Don't wait until a situation has reached the point of no return before you contact the parent.* If a child is not following directions, is failing to complete homework or class work, or is misbehaving, do not let too much time elapse before you contact the parent. Many parents are offended when they show up for parent–teacher conferences and hear a litany of negative comments about their child when they assumed that the child was doing well in class.

4. *Present the parent with a balanced picture of his or her child.* Every teacher needs to be able to tell parents about the good things that a child has done, the areas where the child is doing well, and not just focus on a child's academic weaknesses and the areas where the child is doing poorly. Explain the positives as well as the areas that need improvement.

5. *Try not to be defensive.*

6. *Do not talk down to parents.* Keep in mind that your goal should be to communicate with the parent in a clear and easy-to-understand manner. Don't use academic jargon or language that suggests that you are merely trying to impress or intimidate the parent with your knowledge and extensive vocabulary.

7. *Try to put yourself in the parent's shoes.* Being empathetic is one of the best ways to improve relations with people.

8. *Use mistakes as teachable-moment opportunities.*

9. *Don't blame all African American parents for any negative experiences that you have with a few.*

10. Read *Beyond the Bake Sale: The Essential Guide to Family-School Partnerships* by Anne T. Henderson, Karen L. Mapp, Vivian R. Johnson, and Don Davies.[15] This book is loaded with useful information and wonderful strategies to help educators improve their relations with parents.

11. *Have a list of resources available (local tutoring programs, online resources, etc.) as reference tools for parents with weak skills.*

GROUP ACTIVITY FOR PROFESSIONAL DEVELOPMENT AND COURSE WORK

1. As a group, brainstorm specific ways that you can increase African American parent participation at a local school.

2. Create a forum that will allow you to invite African American parents to share their ideas with you about how teachers can improve their relations with African American students and parents.

3. Each group member can read one chapter of *Beyond the Bake Sale* and summarize the main ideas for the rest of the group.

4. Make a list of resources (local tutoring programs, online resources, etc.) that might be helpful to African American parents.

PART II

*The Curriculum,
Classroom Management,
and Testing*

5

A Hard Knock Life

How Teachers Can Use the Curriculum to Empower African American Students

In November 2008, shortly before I was scheduled to give a presentation to a group of middle school teachers in Florida, I heard a series of comments that alarmed me. At the time, I was going over my presentation notes in the staff workroom. My thoughts were interrupted by the voice of an angry teacher who was speaking to two of her colleagues. "She wanted to know why he has a D in my class!" the teacher declared. "I told her, 'He has a D because he's in sixth grade and he can't read, and he has no support at home!'" Because I'd been invited to the school to describe ways in which teachers could increase their efficacy with African American students, I suspected that she was referring to a black student. Later, another teacher informed me that he was indeed a black student.

The disgruntled teacher clearly had a right to be angry. Evidently, she felt defensive because someone—possibly a school administrator—had questioned the low grade that she'd given to the student. The problem that I had was that she was making a very common mistake that many educators make:

She was focusing on the *inalterable variables*. Before I explain what I mean by this term, I'd like you to complete the following exercise.

EXERCISE 5A: ALTERABLE VERSUS INALTERABLE VARIABLES

Please answer each question as honestly as possible.

1. What are three aspects of students' lives that you can't control?

    _____

    _____

    _____

2. What are three aspects of students' lives that you can control?

    _____

    _____

    _____

★　★　★　★　★

I asked you to complete the previous exercise for two reasons: First, I wanted you to differentiate between alterable and inalterable variables. The term *alterable variables* refers to the aspects of students' lives that teachers can control, and the term has been used by educators and researchers for decades.[1] In her article "Improving Graduation Results: Strategies for Addressing Today's Needs," Camilla Lehr referred to alterable variables as *interventions,* or actions that educators take to decrease drop-out rates, such as improving the "quality of the student–teacher relationship," "instructional practices," and the quality of parent–teacher relations.[2] Judith Stull, of the Temple University Center for Research in Human Development and Education, stated that the Framework for Alterable Variables that was developed during the 1980s has six categories. The five categories that pertain specifically to teachers include the way that teachers teach, what they teach, their classroom management skills, the ways in which teachers interact with students, and "the social-psychological climate of the classroom."[3]

Inalterable variables are the aspects of students' lives over which teachers have no control. Among these are students' socioeconomic level, home life, disability, age, gender, ethnicity, native language, mobility, region of residence, and so on.[4]

I asked you to complete Exercise 5A because I wanted you to realize how powerful you are. Although K–12 educators are overworked, underpaid, often misunderstood, and even disrespected, as an educator, you are one of the most powerful individuals on earth. As I explained in some of my previous books and in Chapter 1 of this book, most children in the United States will spend a considerable amount of time in K–12 classrooms, listening to teachers, interacting with teachers, and forming opinions about themselves that are based on the labels that teachers place on them. The following e-mail, which I received in February of 2009 from one of my former students, illustrates this point.

February 05, 2009

Excuse me, it's Dr. Thompson now. I am so happy to have found you. I think about you all the time. You were my favorite teacher through all my years of school and had the biggest impact on my life. Even when I used to ditch my other classes, I made sure I came to your class. The quotes you use to put on the board were the highlight of my day. I still tell everyone you are the reason I got into real estate.

One day I came to class and you had a quote on the board that said: "He who controls the land controls the wealth, and he who controls the wealth controls the power." I still remember you telling me I had the power to be like Hitler and it was up to me to use that power for good or evil. Those two things had the biggest impact on my life. I am working on a television show to educate and teach people how to overcome any challenge and start their own business. . . .

Here is my e-mail and phone number. I would love to talk to you when you get some time. You had my sister Carla, brother Carl, and [me] in your classes. . . . I was there in "90"–"91" I believe.

Peace and Love,
Niecey (not her real name)

You can imagine how surprising and heartwarming it was for me to hear from this student nearly 20 years after she had been in my class. I laughed when she mentioned what I told her about using her power for good or for evil because, although I didn't remember having made that comment, it sounded like something that I would have said. But more than anything, her e-mail reminded me that teachers can have a positive effect on students without even realizing the short- or even long-term outcomes.

Now, I would like for you to read a story about another teacher and one of her African American students. My goal in sharing this story is, once again, to remind you of two points: (1) You are very powerful, and (2) when you choose to focus on the alterable variables—the factors within your control—you can make a long-term impact on students.

LANETTE'S STORY

LaNette, an African American child, grew up with her five siblings in San Diego, California. When she was still in elementary school, her parents separated, and eventually divorced. After the separation, LaNette and her siblings only saw their father occasionally, and their mother had to go on welfare in order to support her family.

Trying to keep the bills paid, her children clothed and fed, and a roof over their heads was stressful enough for LaNette's mother. But her struggle was compounded by the fact that when she was pregnant with her fifth child, a knife-wielding man whose face was covered by a stocking cap broke into her home, attacked her, and blinded her in her left eye. From this point on, she and her children lived in fear. At home, the children were also routinely subjected to physical, emotional, and verbal abuse.

At the time when her mother was assaulted, LaNette was in kindergarten. Although she had a difficult year at school, when the school term ended her teacher promoted her to first grade. In first grade, like kindergarten, LaNette often cried at school because school was one of the few places where she felt it was safe to release some of the emotional pain that she carried. Therefore, at the end of the school year, the teacher told her mother that LaNette was too immature for second grade.

Having to spend a second year in first grade was one of the most embarrassing experiences of LaNette's life. At home, two of her sisters constantly reminded her that she was "too dumb to pass first grade." At school, she knew that if she continued to cry about all of the pain that was bottled up inside of her, she might be stuck in first grade for a third year. So LaNette found another way to express her emotional pain: She became an excessive talker. The plan worked because, at the end of her second year in first grade, she was promoted to second grade.

For the next few years, LaNette had a series of very negative school experiences. Although she had learned to control her tears at school, the excessive talking got her into lots of trouble because most teachers hate "excessive talkers." In third grade, her teacher punished her by making her stand in the front of the classroom with a wedge of cardboard in her mouth. In fourth grade, the teacher made her stand in the coat closet. In fifth grade, her teacher kept her after school. But none of these punishments stopped her from talking excessively, and nothing convinced any of her teachers that she was anything more than a low-income black child who had little, if any, academic potential. The teachers had low expectations of her, and so did her mother and siblings.

The low expectations that LaNette faced at school and at home could have resulted in a predictable outcome: She could have eventually dropped out of school; she could have eventually been kicked out of school for being viewed as a chronic discipline problem; or like so many other African American K–12 students in similar predicaments, she could have been passed through the school system with weak academic skills and eventually been given a diploma. This pattern was broken by what LaNette later viewed as "divine intervention."

In sixth grade, LaNette was blessed to have the teacher who changed her life. In one year, Mrs. Susan Tessem, a feisty young blonde from suburbia, was able to change the mindset and academic performance of a child who had been written off by the education system. Unlike most of the white teachers at the elementary school, Mrs. Tessem had high expectations, she believed that African American students—regardless of their background—deserved a quality education, and she believed that it was her job to give them the best education that she could. She made the curriculum interesting and relevant, and she made it clear to students that she cared about their academic and overall well-being. Needless to say, LaNette learned more during this year of school than she had in all of her previous years combined. On the last day of school, Mrs. Tessem made it clear to her that she expected LaNette to go to college. From that point on, attending college became one of LaNette's main goals. She believed that after all Mrs. Tessem had done for her, the least that she could do was to fulfill this mission.

After she graduated from sixth grade, LaNette's family moved to another neighborhood, which meant that she no longer lived within walking distance of her elementary school. Although she wasn't able to visit Mrs. Tessem, she never forgot her. In fact, for many years, she dreamed of graduating from college and one day returning to her former elementary school to thank Mrs. Tessem for being the only elementary school teacher who believed that she had the potential to be academically successful.

Many years passed from the time that Mrs. Tessem told LaNette to attend college. LaNette not only earned a bachelor's degree, she eventually earned a teaching credential, a master's degree, and even a doctorate. Throughout the years, she looked for Mrs. Tessem on numerous occasions but was always told that she no longer lived in the United States, and no one seemed to have her address. Nevertheless, LaNette modeled her own teaching style after Mrs. Tessem's and used many of the culturally relevant strategies that Mrs. Tessem used with her own students. Therefore, although Mrs. Tessem didn't actually see the fruit of her hard work, her hard work paid off anyway.

EXERCISE 5B: REFLECTING ON LANETTE'S STORY

Please answer each question as honestly as possible.

1. How can you use LaNette's story to increase your efficacy with African American students?

   _____

   _____

2. Why was Mrs. Tessem more successful with LaNette than her previous elementary school teachers had been?

   _____

   _____

3. If you had a chance to interview LaNette, what would you ask her?

   _____

   _____

4. If you had a chance to interview Mrs. Tessem, what would you ask her?

   _____

   _____

5. As an educator, in what ways are you similar to Mrs. Tessem?

   _____

   _____

6. As an educator, in what ways are you different from Mrs. Tessem?

   _____

   _____

★ ★ ★ ★ ★

UPDATING LANETTE'S STORY

Unlike the stories that you've read in previous chapters of this book, LaNette's story wasn't shared with me by one of my former students, acquaintances, friends, parents, or educators. It's actually *my* story. LaNette is my middle name, and the story that you read describes my childhood and the teacher who changed my life. In the chapter called "How Can Teachers Reach African American Students From Challenging

Backgrounds?" in *Through Ebony Eyes: What Teachers Need to Know but Are Afraid to Ask About African American Students,* I also shared my story and wrote extensively about Mrs. Tessem, my sixth-grade teacher.

Since that book was published in 2004, I have given presentations to thousands of educators and retold the story. The main reason why I constantly retell this story is that I want teachers to truly believe that they can change their students' lives. I also share the story because I want educators to realize that their students—especially African Americans from challenging backgrounds—have the potential to become just as successful as I have become.

Over the past five years, many educators have asked me questions about Mrs. Tessem that I wasn't able to answer. Unfortunately, I spent more than 30 years trying to find her in order to thank her for making such a powerful impact on my life. After so much time had passed without my being able to locate her, I finally gave up and concluded that Mrs. Tessem must have died. Nevertheless, I never stopped thinking about her and telling educators about her.

In September 2008, I gave an acceptance speech at a reception where I received an Award of Distinction from the Black Graduate Students' Association at the university where I work. At the beginning of the speech, I mentioned that one of my biggest regrets was that I had never been able to thank the teacher who changed the course of my life. Later, one of my African American doctoral students read the chapter of *Through Ebony Eyes* in which I described Mrs. Tessem. A few days after this student read the chapter and heard me speak about Mrs. Tessem, she sent me an e-mail that let me know that miracles do indeed happen, for it contained Mrs. Tessem's contact information.

When I finally spoke to Mrs. Tessem by telephone, she told me that when she received my first voicemail, she had only been in the United States for a few hours. Furthermore, she would only be in the United States for a few more days before returning to Central America. Two days later, my husband, Rufus, and I drove to the coastal California town where she was visiting a friend, and I finally got the chance that I'd been waiting for. The first thing I noticed was that she still had the same beautiful smile that I'd always remembered. She was also still blonde and looked much younger than I'd expected. To my delight, she was still just as feisty, straightforward, and down-to-earth as I'd remembered.

For the next few hours, we spoke about the impact that she'd had on me and my gratitude toward her, and she also answered the questions that I hadn't been able to answer about her teaching philosophy. The interview that she allowed me to conduct with her confirmed a lot of my suspicions and validated many of the conclusions that I have drawn about good teachers—especially effective teachers of African American students. But I also learned many new details that I hadn't known about Mrs. Tessem, such as where and how she grew up and what she has been doing since she emigrated to Central America. In the next section, I share what I learned, and after you read "An Interview With Mrs. Tessem," I'll ask you to complete a related exercise.

AN INTERVIEW WITH MRS. TESSEM: "I WANTED TO BE A GOOD TEACHER."

Mrs. Tessem grew up with her parents and brother in a family that valued education. Her mother, a third-grade teacher, and her father, a college professor and later a dean, were "encouraging parents" who taught her to be "community oriented" and instilled strong religious values in her. Being respectful and having integrity were two of the most important values that her parents believed in. During the period when her father was earning his doctorate, Mrs. Tessem attended an excellent elementary school that was housed at the prestigious university that her father attended. At this elementary school, her teachers made a strong, positive impact on her and used a "discovery" method of teaching. "We had to figure it out," she explained. "That is the challenging part of it; get them [the students] to figure it out."

The good teaching models that Mrs. Tessem witnessed at a young age, through her parents and exemplary teachers of her own, had a strong effect on her. "I really respected what my parents were doing," she stated. "Some of the choices for women were limited at that time. Women were teachers or nurses. [Being a teacher] was what I wanted to be."

After earning her teaching credential, she secured a job at a predominantly white, affluent elementary school in southern California. At this school, she used some of the same methods that she'd learned from her mother and her best teachers. "I think that when I first started," she explained, "I wanted to be a good teacher. I decided if I couldn't be a good teacher, I wouldn't be worth the powder to blow me up with! Teaching is a noble profession." The principal of the school was supportive, and "taught me how important the lesson plans were, to help [me] think through the process [of what I wanted to teach]" she said. "I just automatically thought that not doing [lesson plans] was a big no-no."

Because of a marriage proposal, which she accepted, Mrs. Tessem only remained at the predominantly white, affluent school for one year. Her acceptance of the marriage proposal meant that she would have to relocate to another southern California city in order to be near her husband. But relocating and being a newlywed were the least of her worries. It turned out that when she applied for a teaching job, she was assigned to an underperforming, predominantly black, low-income elementary school. "At first, when I got my assignment," she said, "I went down to the employment office and said, 'I think this is a terrible mistake.' They said, 'No. You can put in for a transfer in December,' and 'this is where they put the new teachers.' Before that, I knew no colored people. I actually thought that this was a mistake, that I wasn't qualified." At the time, Mrs. Tessem was only 24 years old.

So she started her new job with the belief that it would only be a temporary situation and that she'd be able to transfer to a better school in December. The predominantly black school was plagued by a culture of low teacher expectations. According to Mrs. Tessem, "There were too many teachers looking at the advantages of being able to sit and do nothing, pass out worksheets, not do lesson plans. It was just horrible. I think that some of the teachers who were poor teachers in that environment would have been poor teachers in any environment."

Instead of adopting the same attitude of low expectations that was prevalent at the school, Mrs. Tessem decided to do her best. "I didn't have much respect for some of the other teachers," she said. "I would get furious with the low expectations." So Mrs. Tessem did what she had done the previous year. She explained, "I think that I would have been exactly the same if I had been at an all-white school because I was at an all-white school and I did exactly the same thing." That "thing" was doing the best that she could to help students rise to the level of her expectations and using the curriculum to empower her students.

In the back of her new classroom, she posted a sign that had her picture on it. The sign said, "Mrs. Tessem is not always right, but she's always boss." On the first day of school, "I decided to sing the 'Star Spangled Banner,' and I ended up singing alone," she said. Then, she explained her expectations, saying, "I expect you to be here, earn at least a C, and respect me."

Her first week at the school was challenging. When she told one student to stop bouncing a ball in the classroom, he declared, "You're nothing more than a [N-word] hater!" Instead of overreacting as many teachers might have done, Mrs. Tessem said that she merely replied, "No, I'm not." Then, she turned around and continued to do her work. "And he never bounced the ball in class again." On another occasion, according to Mrs. Tessem, a girl told her, "You're nothing more than a [%$%#%$# N-word] hater!" "And I said, 'If you think about it, that's impossible.' That was the end of that matter." When I asked Mrs. Tessem if she was ever fearful of working in a predominantly black, low-income school and community, she replied, "No. One day, somebody got mad at me and called me a 'skinny bag of bones,' and I said, 'Oh. Thank you!' I never had any fear; it was just part of me."

Long before December arrived, Mrs. Tessem had decided that she wouldn't request a transfer after all. She had a supportive principal, and more important, she was seeing positive results in her students. They were learning what she was trying to teach them. "I just enjoyed the reaction that I got," she explained. "And the progress that was being made, the students' ability to be able to express themselves orally, in writing, in the chorus, in the plays, and [for them to realize] that they were better than they thought that they could be." Although she wasn't "a music person," Mrs. Tessem started a chorus at the school, which became very popular. She did this because at her previous teaching job, she had been asked to work with the chorus. So at the new school, since there was already a piano in the classroom, she did the same thing. She asked a talented pianist in the class to become the regular pianist and started a school-wide program that resulted in her chorus singing at numerous events.

Mrs. Tessem strongly believed that a teacher's main job is "getting that curriculum in your hands and figuring out how to get it across to the kids." When she started working at the predominantly black school, she used the same methods that she had used at the affluent white school. Although she saw that her hard work was paying off, she also believed that she could become even more effective if she learned more about black culture. At that time, the principal of the school offered teachers an opportunity to engage "in dialogues with black leaders in the community," but only Mrs. Tessem and two other teachers accepted the offer. "You were pitted against what the black person was thinking," she recounted, "and that was good because it made you aware."

Her desire to be an exemplary teacher was so great that she decided to go a step further. At the time, she was working on her master's degree in geography, but decided to change her major to black studies. "I was so naïve at that time," she explained, "and I thought I really should look into black studies. I really felt that I needed that preparation. I figured that if I was going to stay [at the elementary school], I'd better know what I was doing." Although she never ended up finishing her thesis on "The Invisibility of the Black Man," she still has her notes, still refers to them periodically, and still uses the information that she learned from black literature and history to better understand people. After all, she stated, "If you look around the world, most of the problems are cultural."

During the seven years that she worked at the predominantly black school, Mrs. Tessem taught many types of students. After several years of teaching regular sixth-grade classes, she was asked to teach the emotionally handicapped students' class. "They asked me to take it. I said, 'I have no background in this.' They said, 'You'll do just fine.'" And of course, she did. Mrs. Tessem was successful with these students because she understood their needs, treated them humanely, and sought to help them perform well academically. In each class, she had 12 students who had previously been confined to cubicles by teachers. However, she eradicated this practice and realized "All these kids had average or above average intelligence, but they had emotional problems." On report card day, she even agreed to go home with students who were terrified that they'd be beaten by a parent if they had earned low grades. She wanted the parents to know that even if the grade didn't reflect progress, the student was indeed making progress.

After seven years of teaching at the predominantly black school, Mrs. Tessem developed a health problem that wouldn't permit her to give "teaching her best effort." She went into a business that her family owned and eventually moved to Central America to run a company that her brother started. At the time when I interviewed her, although she had been away from teaching for 25 years, she still had some very strong beliefs about the teaching profession, students, and U.S. schools. In the exercise that follows, I will share some related quotes from Mrs. Tessem (including a few that I didn't include in the interview summary that you just read) and ask you to respond to them.

EXERCISE 5C: REFLECTING ON "AN INTERVIEW WITH MRS. TESSEM" AND QUOTES FROM MRS. TESSEM

Please respond to each question and quote as honestly as possible.

1. What did you learn from "An Interview With Mrs. Tessem" that can help you increase your efficacy with African American students?

   _____

   _____

2. According to Mrs. Tessem, "Anybody who wants to be a teacher has to realize the nobility of what you're doing on a daily basis." What is your interpretation of this statement? Explain why you agree or disagree with it.

   _____

   _____

3. Mrs. Tessem stated, "Teachers should treat each individual as a precious mind." Explain why you agree or disagree.

   _____

   _____

4. According to Mrs. Tessem, many educators "haven't treated these children with the respect and gentleness that they need." She was referring to African American, low-income students and children in urban communities. Explain why you agree or disagree with her statement.

   _____

   _____

5. Mrs. Tessem believed that her African American students deserved the same quality of education that she had previously given to her affluent white students. Do you

honestly believe that African American students deserve the same quality of education as wealthy white students? Please explain your answer.

_____

_____

6. Do you honestly believe that you could teach a classroom full of African American students with the same sense of commitment and level of expectations that you would have for a predominantly white, affluent class? Please explain your answer.

_____

_____

7. Now, after learning more about Mrs. Tessem and her philosophy about teaching, if you could interview her, what would you ask her or say to her?

_____

_____

8. In Exercise 5B, I asked you to explain how, as an educator, you are similar to or different from Mrs. Tessem. Now that you have learned more about her, what would you change about your previous answers?

_____

_____

★　★　★　★　★

USING THE CURRICULUM TO EMPOWER STUDENTS

Mrs. Tessem was an effective teacher for several reasons. First, she had the correct mindset about her students. Second, she had high expectations for students. Third, she cared about her students' overall well-being. Fourth, she used the curriculum to empower students. In *Through Ebony Eyes* and *Up Where We Belong,* I explained strategies and offered extensive explanations of how teachers can use the curriculum to help students from challenging backgrounds, students of color, and low-performing students. Instead of repeating what I said in those books, in the next section, I will summarize some of the main points about the curriculum and explain eight ways that you can use the curriculum to empower African American students, particularly those who are from challenging backgrounds.

Raise Your Expectations for Yourself

When Mrs. Tessem was first assigned to teach at the predominantly black elementary school that I attended, she went to the employment office and told the official in charge that she believed that a mistake had been made. Ironically, she didn't believe that teaching at the low-income, under-performing school was beneath her, especially since she had previously taught at an affluent, predominantly white school. Instead, she believed that *she was unqualified* to teach at this school because she hadn't had contact with African Americans before, and she hadn't been trained to teach the types of children who attended this school.

Like Mrs. Tessem, many teachers who are hired to work at predominantly black, low-income schools also feel that they aren't qualified to work at these sites. However, few will admit this or even ask for help. In the "Mindset Study," the 237 preservice teachers, teachers, and administrators were asked to respond to the statement, "In my opinion, most teachers know how to work effectively with African American K–12 students." The overwhelming majority (90%) of the respondents said that most teachers don't (see Appendix E). This shockingly high percentage indicates that many teachers desperately need help in increasing their efficacy with African American students.

In Mrs. Tessem's case, when she realized that she needed to learn more information about how to increase her efficacy, she enrolled in graduate-level black literature and black history courses. In your own case, you have already embarked upon the journey toward increasing your efficacy merely by reading the previous chapters of this book and completing the previous exercises. If, however, you are still feeling uncertain about your ability to work effectively with African American students, the following strategies will help you. But before you read the other strategies, I would like you to take some time to reflect upon your own sense of efficacy with African American students, and if you haven't already done so, make up your mind that you can and will be a successful educator of African American students. In other words, your ability to use the curriculum to empower students must first begin with your commitment to become an effective educator of African American students and your decision to raise your expectations for yourself.

Raise Your Expectations for African American Students

As I explained previously, many teachers and principals do not believe that African American students are capable of academic excellence. In fact, in the "Mindset Study," 65% of the preservice teachers, 52% of the teachers, and 48%f of the administrators said that most principals don't believe that most African American K–12 students are capable of doing outstanding academic work. In terms of what teachers believe, 70% of the preservice teachers, 52% of the teachers, and 57% of the administrators said that most teachers don't believe that most African American students are capable of doing outstanding academic work.

The respondents in the "Mindset Study" also answered the question, "What are the main reasons why many African American students do not do as well in school as they could?" The most-frequently cited answer was "low teacher expectations." Sixty-six percent of the preservice teachers, 45% of the teachers, and 53% of the administrators said this. However, even more troubling is that many of the respondents made it clear that most teachers do not believe that African American students are as intelligent as other students. With the exception of males and whites, 50% to 75% of the other subgroups (preservice teachers, teachers, administrators, nonwhites, and females) indicated that most teachers don't believe that black students are as intelligent (see Appendix E).

If you had been asked to respond to this question about your own beliefs, what would you have said? In other words, do you believe that African American students are as intelligent as other students? If you don't, this belief will probably become a self-fulfilling prophecy in your classroom and you will, undoubtedly, foster a climate of low expectations for African American students. Therefore, in order to be able to use the curriculum to empower African American students, you have to believe that they are capable of understanding and mastering the subject matter that you are being paid to teach.

Be Willing to Improve the Way That You Teach

In the "Mindset Study," a substantial percentage of participants also blamed poor teaching methods and a nonculturally relevant curriculum for black students' underachievement. When asked "What are the main reasons why many African American K–12 students underachieve?" nearly half of the respondents blamed poor teaching methods and the curriculum. In order to be an effective teacher of African American students, you must be familiar with the material that you are planning to teach so that you can explain it to students in a way that they can understand.

During the interview that I conducted with Mrs. Tessem, she emphasized that planning lessons ahead of time is very important. This is true. When you clearly know what you plan to teach and how you plan to teach it, and you share your agenda or lesson plan with students ahead of time, it will make your job a lot easier. It will also increase the likelihood that you will be successful. At the very least, you should put a lesson plan on the blackboard or whiteboard each day that explains your goal or objective, the related grade-level standard or state standard that the lesson will target, what students will be expected to do, and their homework assignment.

The previous recommendations that I made, "Raise your expectations for yourself" and "Raise your expectations for African American students," are related to my recommendation to "Be willing to improve the way that you teach" because this means that, on an ongoing basis, you will be on the lookout for information and strategies that will better help you convey the subject matter to your students. However, being willing to improve your teaching also means that you will use diverse teaching methods, a point that I emphasize in the next section.

Make the Curriculum Interesting

As I've said in several of my previous books, *boredom* is one of the main reasons why so many African American students, especially those in the upper elementary grades and in middle and high school, appear to be apathetic. Contrary to popular opinion, these students do want to learn, and teachers who make the curriculum interesting find that this is definitely true. In *African American Teens Discuss Their Schooling Experiences,*[5] the ability to make the curriculum interesting was tied for first place (along with the ability to make the curriculum comprehensible) as a top quality of outstanding educators.

Niecey, my former high school student whose e-mail you read earlier in this chapter, reminded me of how important it is for teachers to make the curriculum interesting. She used to ditch all of her classes—except for mine. When I asked her why, during the telephone conversation that resulted from her e-mail, she said that in her other classes, she didn't feel challenged, the teachers didn't make the curriculum interesting, and there were little, if any, activities that required students to be active versus passive participants. She mentioned how much she enjoyed the discussions that we had in my class, the mock trials, and the projects that she was required to do.

There are two easy ways for you to learn how to make the curriculum interesting to African American students. First, you can simply ask students or other teachers for feedback. A practical way to do this is at the beginning of the school year, preferably during the first week of school, you can ask students to complete an exercise that requires them to (1) make a list of the five best activities or assignments that they have ever had in any class, and (2) write a paragraph about their best teacher and explain the three best teaching strategies that this teacher used. PreK and kindergarten teachers may modify this activity by asking veteran teachers to describe effective strategies that they have used with African American students.

Second, you can take student feedback seriously. When African American students complain about being bored or say that they don't like assignments, this is a great time for you to use this as a *teachable moment* exercise. For example, during the late 1980s, when I realized that many of my junior high school students were bored with the curriculum of my language arts class, I asked students what they would do if they were the teacher in charge and actually gave volunteers an opportunity to earn extra credit by designing lesson plans and teaching them to the class. This activity became so popular that from that year on, I incorporated a "You Be the Teacher" segment into my curriculum, and I continued to use this strategy after I became a high school teacher. Today, several of my former students, including African Americans, have become teachers, and I suspect that the opportunities that I gave them to design lesson plans and to actually teach the class may have played a role in their decision to become teachers.

In order to be an effective teacher of African American students, you must make the curriculum interesting. As Mrs. Tessem said, "You sort of sit around thinking of really great things to do so that the job is enjoyable." If you are willing to do this, not only will students be excited about learning in your class, but you will also find that your job is a lot more enjoyable.

Make the Curriculum Comprehensible

As I said in the previous section, the ability to make the curriculum interesting and the ability to make the curriculum comprehensible are two of the most important qualities that African American students associate with good teaching. As I often say to educators during the workshops that I conduct, "If the students aren't understanding what you're saying, then you are merely teaching to the walls!"

Making the curriculum comprehensible requires using diverse teaching strategies. Instead of over-relying on lecturing, good teachers tell relevant stories to illustrate points, and they allow students to collaborate with a partner or in small groups, engage regularly in class discussions, create posters and projects, give presentations, and learn to conduct research. Using the arts to teach is also important.

One of the main ways to ascertain whether or not students comprehend the subject matter is to do frequent checks for understanding. Asking students whether or not they understand the information throughout your lecture or presentation won't suffice. Some students are too shy or too embarrassed to admit that they don't understand the information. Asking volunteers to paraphrase the main points is a more effective strategy. Asking students to find a partner and explain the main points is another. Having students write a one-paragraph summary of the main ideas, take quizzes, and play games that are designed to help them review the important information on which they will be tested are activities that can allow them to demonstrate what they know.

Make the Curriculum Relevant

In order to be an effective teacher of African American students, you must also make the curriculum relevant. For decades, many researchers have emphasized that there is a link between what is taught, how it is taught, and African American underachievement. Feedback from students corroborates this point. In *Up Where We Belong*, a substantial percentage of the African American and Latino students who participated in the study on which that book is based said that the curriculum wasn't teaching them what they needed to know in order to survive in their communities or even in the "real world." In a January 2009 article in the *Claremont Courier*, the main newspaper for the city in which I work, Monica Almond, one of my African American graduate students (and the very student who tracked down Mrs. Tessem for me), wrote about the importance of a relevant curriculum that African American students can relate to. In explaining why attending the inauguration of President Barack Obama was so important to her, Monica shared many details about her childhood in affluent, predominantly white communities in Orange County, California. According to Monica:

> I went to school and church with people from a different world—majority White and well off. Many times I was the only Black child in my class, sometimes in the entire grade. As a young Black girl, from a family of 6, it was difficult for me to consciously befriend my White friends of greater means and reputation. There was a persistent feeling of inadequacy and illegitimacy as I read textbooks of American heroes, authors, and inventors that looked nothing like me. It was rare to hear stories about the countless unsung African American heroes who, through their blood, sweat, and tears, helped to make this country what it is today. I yearned to know more about my people and what made us great.[6]

Monica's words underscore the fact that all students need to feel a personal connection to the curriculum that is taught in school, and all children need to learn about the contributions made by people from their racial background. When this connection is lacking, the sense of inadequacy and illegitimacy that she spoke of can lead to disinterest, or even open resistance to a curriculum that students might view as irrelevant.

Although there is a substantial body of research on culturally relevant teaching,[7] during my travels, I often meet teachers who still have difficulty finding ways to make the curriculum interesting and relevant. The bottom line is that in order to be an effective teacher of African American students, you must find ways to make the curriculum relevant. In other words, the curriculum has to consist of strategies and information that students can use on a short-term and long-term basis.

One of the easiest ways to make the curriculum relevant is to teach students problem-solving skills. This is something that Dr. Janice Hale highly recommends for teachers of African American students.[8] When teachers equip students with tools to deal with common life problems, such as bullying, racism, discrimination, abuse, and so on, they are truly making the curriculum relevant. Without repeating what I've said in my previous books about how teachers can make the curriculum relevant, I will offer a few suggestions here. Having students discuss a problem such as racism, write about it, brainstorm solutions, conduct related research, and create related projects are ways that you can make the curriculum relevant and empower students at the same time. When students are permitted to do assignments that are related to the problems that they face or that are common in their community, you will see for yourself how desperate and eager African American students are to *learn* new information and to participate in class activities.

Another way that you can make the curriculum relevant and empower students at the same time is to commission them to become detectives. Having students list problems that concern them, select one topic for research purposes, and collect data are ways that this can be done. Using the arts is another way that you can make the curriculum interesting and relevant, as well as give students creative ways to demonstrate that they understand the subject matter. Having students write about music that is related to the main ideas of the subject matter they need to know and having them create original songs that are related to the subject matter that you are teaching are two ways that you can use music in your lesson plans. Students can also draw and paint posters and create their own book versions of the main ideas and themes that they are expected to understand from the literature and textbooks that they read.

Help Students Improve Their Academic Skills

Obviously, the main purpose of the curriculum is for students to learn important information and skills that they need in order to be successful in school and after they leave school. At the very least, all students need good reading, writing, and mathematics skills in order to do well academically. However, because of low expectations from other teachers, many of your African American students may be performing below grade level in these areas when they are assigned to your class. Regardless of their skill level when they arrive, it is your professional obligation to do everything that you can to help them reach and, ideally, surpass grade level standards by the end of the academic year.

In terms of reading, it is important that students can decode and comprehend the subject matter that they need to know in your class. If an upper-elementary level student or secondary student cannot decode words, it is important that you request assistance from the school or district-level reading specialist because this student will need intensive one-on-one assistance. Allowing students to discuss what they've read in literature and from textbooks as a class, with a partner, or in small groups are ways that you can ascertain whether or not they comprehend what they read before they are tested on reading assignments. Having students write about reading assignments is another way.

As I've repeatedly said in most of the other books that I've written, "Writing is one of the most neglected areas of the curriculum." In spite of this, all students need to have good writing skills, and teachers who fail to devote adequate time to writing instruction and assigning writing tasks are doing them a great disservice. Having students write frequently, giving them written feedback about their work, giving them opportunities to revise and improve their work, and showing them samples of good writing—essays, business letters, research papers, and so on—will help students develop skills that will benefit them on a short- and long-term basis.

I have also written and spoken extensively about the main reasons why many African American K–12 students struggle with math, particularly algebra. The bottom line is that most students can do well at math. According to Dr. David E. Drew, a math expert and the author of *Aptitude Revisited,* math is one of the main areas in which African American students and females have been shortchanged by the U.S. education system as a result of low expectations and stereotypes about their ability to master math.[9]

In order to help African American students develop good math skills, you must (1) believe that the students are capable and (2) ensure that students have mastered the basics—addition, subtraction, multiplication, division, the rules governing working with signed numbers, and so on—before expecting students to do higher-level math problems.

Help Students Understand How They Can Use the Curriculum for Personal Empowerment

In a previous section of this chapter, I urged you to use feedback from African American students—especially complaints—as an opportunity to improve the curriculum. But there are at least two other ways that you can use feedback from students: (1) to dash their dreams or to give them hope and (2) to understand and address any special challenges that a student might be facing.

In terms of destroying dreams or giving students hope, many teachers don't realize how much power they actually wield over students, or that they have been guilty of destroying dreams. In a previous chapter, I shared Nathan's story with you. In his case, a nun, Sister Mary P., and other educators destroyed his desire to learn in the school system. Another example that comes to mind is a story that an African American educator told me about her brother. When he was a little boy, he told his kindergarten or first grade teacher that he wanted to be a lawyer or a pilot when he grew up. Instead of encouraging this child and giving him hope, the teacher told him that black people couldn't be pilots or lawyers. Because an adult told him this, the child believed it. From then on, he decided that he could never pursue either of those professions. Before long, the boy had become an underachiever who was viewed by teachers as problematic. After a very negative K–12 school experience, he eventually went into the military. Over time, he realized that his teacher had been wrong: Black people can become attorneys. So he enrolled in and graduated from law school much later in life than he would have if his teacher hadn't lied to him years ago. In 2009, he was in his 50s and planning to take the bar exam.

You can also use the curriculum to uncover and address any special challenges that students might be facing. When students are permitted to write about personal experiences in essays, journals, and other assignments, you can learn a lot about their personal lives. However, you can also be proactive; instead of waiting until you read or hear about a traumatic event that a student has experienced, you can incorporate *resiliency-building* strategies into the curriculum on a regular basis. For example, during my years as a junior high school and high school teacher, I constantly told stories about individuals who overcame adversity; had students read stories about individuals who overcame adversity; had them brainstorm, write about, and discuss the ways that various individuals handled adversity; and shared my own personal story and the strategies that I used with them.

In *Resiliency: What We Have Learned*, Bonnie Benard emphasized that the main difference between children from challenging backgrounds who turned out well as adults and those who didn't was that most of the children who turned out well had at least one "turnaround person" in their lives. By "turnaround person," she meant a powerful, influential, life-changing adult who made a positive impact on the child. In the case of educators, according to Benard, turnaround teachers:

- have high expectations for students,
- have a strengths-based versus deficit-based perspective of students,
- give students multiple opportunities to participate in class,
- permit students to collaborate with other students,
- allow students to discuss and write about the issues that concern them,
- permit students to share their views and voice their concerns,
- form caring relationships with students,
- allow students to share their personal stories orally and through writing,
- incorporate the arts into the curriculum,
- have fair rules and expectations, and
- serve as "informal mentors."[10]

Hopefully, reading this chapter has helped you to realize that you can use the curriculum to help African American students improve their academic skills and also to develop skills that can help them outside of the classroom. When students come from challenging backgrounds, like my own impoverished and abusive background, they need a curriculum that will help them to be academically successful and one that will increase the likelihood that their adulthood will be brighter than their childhood. In my case for example, by telling me to go to college, Mrs. Tessem instilled in me a mindset that made it likely that I would eventually escape from poverty. The seed that she planted in my mind became a part of her efforts to transform me from low-achiever to high-achiever. Like Mrs. Tessem, you will have many opportunities to use the curriculum to empower students, especially students who come from challenging backgrounds; like Mrs. Tessem, you can become a dream-builder. The last exercise in this chapter is designed to help you synthesize the main points that you've learned and to brainstorm additional ways that you can use the curriculum to empower students.

EXERCISE 5D: REFLECTING ON WHAT YOU HAVE LEARNED

Please answer each question as honestly as possible.

1. As an educator, what are your three main expectations of yourself regarding your African American students?

_____

_____

_____

2. What are your three main expectations of your African American students?

_____

_____

_____

3. How do you plan to improve your teaching style so that you will be more effective with African American students?

_____

_____

_____

4. How do you plan to make your lesson plans more interesting?

_____

_____

_____

5. How do you plan to make the curriculum comprehensible?

_____

_____

_____

6. How do you plan to make the curriculum more relevant to African American students?

_____

_____

_____

7. How do you plan to use the curriculum to specifically empower students from challenging backgrounds?

_____

_____

_____

★   ★   ★   ★   ★

GROUP ACTIVITY FOR PROFESSIONAL DEVELOPMENT AND COURSE WORK

Each group member can create a culturally relevant lesson plan, model it to the group, and ask for feedback.

Only the Strong Survive

Dealing With Roadblocks to Effective Classroom Management

In Part 1, I emphasized that in order to be an effective educator of African American students, you must be willing to

- face and address your mental baggage, such as any stereotypes, biases, and racist beliefs that you have about African American students and their parents;
- improve your relations with African American parents; and
- use the curriculum to not only improve students' academic skills but also to empower students, especially those from challenging backgrounds.

However, being an effective educator of African American students also requires that you manage your classroom well. So in this chapter, I share stories and strategies pertaining to classroom management. But first, I'd like you to complete the following related exercise:

EXERCISE 6A: IDENTIFYING YOUR CLASSROOM MANAGEMENT STRENGTHS AND WEAKNESSES

Please respond to each statement or question as honestly as possible.

1. In your opinion, how strong are your classroom management skills? Please explain your answer.

_____

_____

2. What are your main class rules?

_____

_____

3. How do you ensure that all students know and understand your class rules?

_____

_____

4. How do you ensure that you are treating all students fairly?

_____

_____

5. What, if any, classroom management problems have you had with African American students?

_____

_____

6. Please review your answers to the previous questions. Explain what they reveal about your classroom management strengths and weaknesses.

_____

_____

★　★　★　★　★

CRIES FOR HELP: LISTENING TO TEACHERS' EXPERIENCES AND CONCERNS ABOUT CLASSROOM MANAGEMENT

Although teachers can't be effective without good classroom management skills, many teachers struggle in this area—especially new teachers. The following classroom management problems were shared with me through letters written by new teachers who were enrolled in the teacher education program at the university where I work. After you read these excerpts, I'll ask you to complete a related exercise.

A new middle school teacher wrote:

I am having a problem maintaining complete classroom discipline. It seems I will gain control and maintain it only for a little while. Then, I feel like I have to start all over again, wasting class time, lecturing to the students about the classroom rules. Being a brand new 7th grade teacher, I was hoping that classroom management becomes easier. I am so tired of having to always remind my students of the rules. I know they know them.

I have a problem with one of my students not caring about his grade in my class. It seems that this student doesn't care about anything. [During] my first run-in with him, I disciplined him and nothing changed.

Another new teacher wrote:

I have a student who was, at the beginning, a favorite of mine. She is intelligent and interested in English and poetry. Recently, she has turned on me in a very big way. She challenges everything I say. Last Friday, she asked me, "Are you trying to be the kind of teacher everybody hates?"

I'm trying hard not to let her get to me, but as of today, I realized that this has become a power struggle. Today, she was trying to direct the class, saying, "Let's move on. We're not getting anything out of this." I reminded her that I'm in charge, but perhaps I should have just ignored her. I think the reason this is getting to me is that I don't understand why she has started to do this.

I know I have to stop letting it get to me, but I'm not sure how. I'm worried that if I don't shut this down soon, I will lose the class. Should I just ignore her?

A high school teacher wrote:

How do you deal with a class that literally prevents you from teaching? I have a class of very immature, irresponsible, lazy juniors. It appears as if they don't know basic classroom procedures like raising your hand to speak, following directions, being on task, etc. Maybe these aren't universal procedures anymore. I'm not sure.

My challenge is that I use another teacher's room for this class, so it makes me feel out of control. I don't have anywhere I can post my rules and expectations, or other important information. Help!

EXERCISE 6B: REFLECTING ON THE NEW TEACHERS' CRIES FOR HELP

Please respond to each statement as honestly as possible.

1. Which excerpt was most similar to experiences that you've had?

_____

_____

2. In what, if any, way did any of these new teachers contribute to his or her classroom management problems?

_____

_____

3. Which teacher would you feel most comfortable giving advice to, and what advice would you give him or her?

_____

_____

4. Which teacher would you have the most difficulty giving advice to, and why?

_____

_____

★ ★ ★ ★ ★

IT'S NOT JUST NEW TEACHERS: MANY TEACHERS NEED HELP WITH CLASSROOM MANAGEMENT

Although new teachers wrote the excerpts that you just read, new teachers aren't the only educators who struggle with classroom management. In fact, some veteran teachers have such weak classroom management skills that their only solution is to kick students out of class. Sending students to the office is definitely warranted at times, but for some teachers, sending students—especially African Americans—to the office is the *only* classroom management strategy that they use.

The National Center for Education Statistics (NCES) has published some interesting information regarding how discipline problems affect teacher satisfaction rates. The 2007 *Digest of Education Statistics* report, "Teachers' Perceptions About Serious Problems in Their Schools," revealed the following:

- Twenty-three percent of the public secondary school teachers, and nearly 10% of elementary school teachers, said that student tardiness was a serious problem at their school.

- Whereas less than 2% of elementary school teachers viewed "cutting class" by students as a serious problem, nearly 15% of secondary school teachers did.
- Thirty percent of secondary school teachers, and nearly 10% of elementary school teachers, said that student apathy was a serious problem at their school.
- Nearly 34% of secondary school teachers, and nearly 24% of elementary school teachers, said that students' arriving at school "unprepared to learn" was a serious problem.
- Seventeen percent of the secondary school teachers, and 9% of the elementary school teachers, said that "verbal abuse of teachers" was a serious problem at their school.
- Nearly 30% of the secondary school teachers, and nearly 20% of the elementary school teachers, said that "student disrespect for teachers" was a serious problem at their school.[1]

In another report, "Schools and Staffing Survey," the NCES described the factors that are associated with whether or not teachers decide to stay at their current school site, transfer to another school site, or leave the teaching profession entirely. During the 2003–2004 school year, teachers who agreed that "the level of student misbehavior in this school (such as noise and horseplay or fighting in the halls, cafeteria, or student lounge) interferes with my teaching" were more likely to transfer to another school or leave the teaching profession entirely.[2]

The aforementioned research is informative. However, the NCES statistics pertaining to suspension and expulsion rates may be the best place to look at why classroom management is such an important topic for educators to examine.

According to the 2007 *Digest of Education Statistics,* in 2004, more than one million white students, more than one million black students, and over 500,000 Hispanic students were suspended from U.S. public schools.[3] However, these numbers don't tell the whole story. Because more than half of the public school students in the United States are white, and black students only account for about 16% of the student population, one million suspended black students cannot be viewed in the same way as one million suspended white students. In others words, black students are more likely to be suspended from school than any other group of students. Whereas whites accounted for approximately 5% of the suspended students, and Hispanics accounted for nearly 7%, black students accounted for 15%.[4] Expulsion rates were similar, in that black students were more likely to be expelled from school than any other group.[5]

In *Through Ebony Eyes* and *Up Where We Belong,* I wrote extensively about some of the main reasons that African American students, especially males, are more likely to be perceived as discipline problems by teachers than any other group of students. The following list summarizes a number of the reasons why some African American students may misbehave at school:

The reasons why some African American students misbehave in class include the following:

- to let the teacher know that the student doesn't like the teacher's teaching style;
- to inform the teacher that the student believes that the teacher views the student negatively;
- to let the teacher know that the student believes that the teacher is racist;
- to hide the fact that the student is confused about what the teacher is trying to teach;
- to hide the fact that the student has a serious academic weakness;
- to inform the teacher that he/she has not earned the student's respect because the teacher has weak classroom management skills;
- because personal problems, such as abuse or neglect at home, might manifest themselves through misbehavior at school; and
- to retaliate against a teacher whom the student feels has singled him/her out and treated the student unfairly.[6]

Clearly, African American students aren't the only students who misbehave at school, and most African American students are well behaved. However, because they are disproportionately represented among the students who are perceived as discipline problems, and who are suspended and expelled from school, many educators believe that most African American students are discipline problems. If you believe this, this is a dangerous stereotype that must be eradicated from your mind.

It's also important for you to understand how your class rules and classroom management style can either exacerbate or ameliorate situations. Moreover, new teachers, experienced teachers, and even veteran teachers can benefit from the strategies that I describe later in this chapter because research has shown that, whereas teachers who have taught for less than 10 years are more likely to say that student misbehavior interferes with their teaching, a substantial percentage of more experienced teachers (34%) and veteran teachers (33%) admitted the same thing.[7] Therefore, the remainder of this chapter consists of stories, strategies, research, and exercises to help you strengthen your classroom management skills and, thereby, increase your efficacy with African American students.

SOME CLASSROOM MANAGEMENT BASICS

1. Deal With Your Fears

Teachers' fear of students, especially African American males, is one of the main reasons why so many African American males are viewed as discipline problems and are suspended, expelled, and tracked for prison. In "Everybody's Intimidated by Us: A Candid Conversation With African

American Males," a chapter of *Up Where We Belong*, many of the black male high school students who participated in the study on which that book is based said that teachers are very fearful of black male students, that teachers look for excuses to kick them out of class, and that teachers confuse hip hop clothing with gang attire. There is a plethora of research that shows that the widespread fear that Americans have about black males continues to cause a great deal of physical, emotional, and psychological pain for black males, and at school, many promising African American males have negative experiences that stem from the fear that educators have about them. In fact, Dr. Jawanza Kunjufu wrote a whole series about this topic.[8] Therefore, as an educator, if you have not dealt with your baggage about black males and any fear that you have about black females—and most educators have not—you will never become as effective with African American students as you have the potential to become.[9]

2. Strengthen Your Assertiveness Skills

Teachers'—especially white, female teachers'—lack of assertiveness is another common reason why so many African American students are labeled as discipline problems at school. If you were socialized to be docile and unassuming, and have not strengthened your assertiveness skills, many African American students will view you as weak and unworthy of respect.[10] When teachers complain that they can't control their classes and that the students are out of control, this is often the main reason why these problems occur.

3. Make Sure That Students Know and Understand Your Class Rules and Expectations

In order to set the right tone about learning and to decrease the likelihood that students will misbehave in class, it is important for you to make sure that students know and understand your class rules—starting on the first day of school. Students need to hear the rules and see the rules on an ongoing basis. The rules should be simple and sensible. When I taught high school, for example, on the first day of school, I explained my class rules and gave students a one-sheet handout that explained my class rules, expectations, and grading policy. I required students to take it home, reread it, sign it, have a parent or guardian sign it, and return it to me before the week ended. Students who met this deadline earned extra credit.

4. Don't Permit Any Student to Keep Other Students From Learning

Some teachers choose to ignore student misbehavior; in so doing, they allow the disruptive student to create distractions that prevent others from concentrating on their work. When a teacher does this, he or she is not only giving the disruptive student permission to continue to misbehave, the teacher is also allowing the disruptive student to shortchange himself or herself, and other students, academically. When a student is disruptive, there are numerous ways that you can respond, but ignoring the situation will only create more problems. Asking the disruptive student to step outside of the classroom so that you can have a private conversation with him or her while the rest of the class is working is a simple way to address the matter quickly and without spectators. It gives you and the disruptive student an opportunity to "save face." During this time, you can ask the student why he or she isn't doing the class work, and you can develop an appropriate plan to remedy the situation based on what the student has said.

5. Don't Show Favoritism

It is human nature for us to like some individuals more than others—and even to dislike some. However, showing favoritism can backfire on teachers in a big way. Showing favoritism can lead to allegations of sexual impropriety, and it can cause other students to accuse the teacher of being biased and unfair and can result in a loss of student respect for the teacher.

6. Deal With Bullying

Bullying is common among adults, adolescents, and children, but it absolutely cannot be tolerated in the classroom. When a child complains to a teacher that one or more students is picking on him or her, as the person who is paid to protect students and to create a classroom environment that is conducive to learning, it is your professional obligation to do something. Many teachers have gotten into the habit of blaming the victim and ignoring the complaints of students who are being verbally and even physically abused by classmates. Sometimes, these situations escalate and cause huge problems that could have been avoided if the teacher had taken the complaints seriously.

7. Don't Allow Students to Use Offensive Language

No student should be permitted to use any offensive language, including racist, stereotypical, or sexist language in class. That includes the "N word." In *Through Ebony Eyes,* I devoted a whole chapter to explaining why teachers shouldn't permit African American students to use the "N word" in class. Many teachers are confused and fearful about how to handle situations that arise, but the bottom line is that no offensive language should be tolerated in the classroom.

8. Don't Make Mountains out of Molehills

Another main reason that many African American students are labeled as discipline problems at school is because often, teachers magnify little problems. When a student engages in normal childish behavior, for example, a teacher may attach greater significance to the behavior than is required, especially if the culprit is an African American boy. In *Bad Boys: Public Schools in the Making of Black Masculinity*, Ann Ferguson described how teachers' fears and stereotypes about black males caused some elementary school teachers to view black boys as if they were adults instead of children. This "adultification" on the part of teachers prompted them to kick children out of class for behaviors that they would not have viewed as serious if nonblack boys had engaged in them.[11] Two of the case studies that you will be examining later in this chapter emphasize why it is so important for you to not overreact to behaviors that should be ignored or minimized.

9. Be Fair

"Fairness" is one of the qualities that African American students equate with outstanding teaching.[12] However, because of their mental baggage about African Americans, many teachers have trouble treating African American students fairly; they find it easier to overreact to the behaviors of African American students by punishing them for behaviors, such as excessive talking, loudness, being off-task, being out of their seat, and so on, that they would ignore or minimize when engaged in by nonblack students. If you will recall, for example, in a previous chapter, I mentioned that one of the findings from the "Mindset Study" was that the overwhelming majority of preservice teachers (82%), teachers (77%), and administrators (72%) said that most teachers do not treat and view African American students in the same ways as nonblack students (see Appendix E).

10. Don't Allow Yourself to Be Treated Disrespectfully

One of the dangers that you have to be aware of in your quest to increase your efficacy with African American students is that of wanting so desperately to do a good job that you allow students to disrespect you. Often, the teachers who fall into this category are those who try to become friends with their students because they want to be liked and popular. I have seen many cases, and actually had a few related experiences when I was a new high school teacher, where I saw this type of scenario backfire on the teacher. In every case where the teacher tried to befriend the students, the teacher ended up being treated disrespectfully, and viewed disdainfully, by students who might once have respected him or her. Not allowing yourself to be disrespected means that you will

- treat students respectfully;
- expect students to treat you respectfully;

- not cross the line by trying to behave as if you were your students' friend or peer;
- keep in mind that you are supposed to behave as if you are the authority figure, the person in charge of the classroom at all times; and
- not tolerate any verbal abuse from any student.

Now that you have read the aforementioned points about classroom management, I'd like you to complete three exercises that are designed to see how well you understood these points. Each exercise will require you to read an actual case study and answer related questions. After you complete each exercise, you'll read an update about the case study and be able to reevaluate your responses.

EXERCISE 6C: REFLECTING ON CASE STUDY 1

Read the following case study, and answer the related questions as honestly as you can.

A Second Grade Teacher's Dilemma

During the 2006–2007 school year, an elementary school teacher in the San Diego Unified School District found herself with a dilemma. She taught at a predominantly black and Latino low-income school, yet this Latina teacher only had one African American child in her class. One day, a Latina student told the teacher that the African American boy had upset her. "Teacher," the girl complained, "he said that I look like I'm going to have a baby."

1. If you were the second-grade teacher, how would you handle this situation?

   _____

   _____

2. If the allegation is indeed true, in your opinion, what might have prompted the African American second grader to say that the girl looked like she was going to have a baby?

   _____

   _____

The case study that you read was actually shared with me by my younger sister. One day, she telephoned me to say that a child had accused her seven-year-old son of saying that she looked like she was going to have a baby. According to my sister, "The girl was fat and had a big stomach." But when the teacher heard the allegation, she said, "Oh, my goodness! That's sexual harassment!" She sent my nephew to the office, his mother was contacted, and a note went into his file that indicated that he had "sexually harassed" another student.

This story alarmed me for two reasons. First, I believed that the teacher had overreacted. More important, however, I was concerned that my nephew would now have a file that could be used to track him into the "school-to-prison pipeline" that I described in the Introduction of this book. In other words, this one allegation could become the basis for teachers to view him as a sexual predator and to overreact to any future comments or behaviors on his part, and that information could one day land him in juvenile hall and, eventually, jail. I urged my sister to transfer him out of that classroom immediately. She was so outraged over how the situation was handled that she ended up transferring him to a different school.

In early 2009, I gave a presentation called "Do You See Obama or Do You See Osama? How Educators Can Help or Harm African American Male Students" to two groups of educators in the Los Angeles Unified School District. I asked the educators to share their thoughts about the case study that you just read. One African American educator asked me what the parent had done to ensure that her child would not make the same mistake again. This woman clearly believed that my nephew was entirely at fault and it was his mother's job to fix the problem. However, most of the other educators who shared their views with the group said that first, they would find out if the boy had made the comment in the first place. Instead of automatically assuming that he was guilty, they would have given him a chance to defend himself. Second, if he admitted that he had indeed made the comment, they would have asked him why he had said it. In other words, they wouldn't have necessarily assumed that he had a negative motive. Instead of engaging in adultification and viewing him as a perverted adult, they would give him the benefit of the doubt.

However, one educator, a white elementary school teacher said, "I would've told the kids to settle it themselves. I don't like for them to come whining to me with tattling." Her comments disturbed me as much as the one by the African American woman who blamed the parent. I informed this woman that it is unwise for an educator to tell children who are too young to have strong conflict-resolution skills to settle a problem that they aren't developmentally ready to handle. I also told her that by telling the children to handle the problem themselves, she could end up getting into serious trouble with a disgruntled parent. What if the girl had gone home and told her parents that "the teacher didn't do anything when I went to her for help"?

Now, I'd like you to compare your responses to those of the other educators whom I just described. Did you (1) automatically assume that the African American boy was guilty? (2) Did you blame the boy's mother? (3) Did you say that you would have told the children to settle the matter on their own? (4) Did you say that you would first seek more information? (5) Did you select an extreme option, like the second-grade teacher actually did?

3. What does the way that you said you would have handled this situation reveal about you, your classroom management skills, and your views of African American boys?

_____

_____

EXERCISE 6D: RESPONDING TO CASE STUDY 2

Read the following case study, and answer the related questions as honestly as you can.

A Sixth Grader's Dilemma

One day, during lunchtime at a middle school in Florida, a black sixth-grade boy asked a staff member for permission to go to the restroom. The staff member told him that he needed to wait until the bell rang. The boy insisted that he had to go anyway. Again, the staff member informed him that he would have to wait until lunchtime was officially over. The student ignored her and left the cafeteria without permission.

1. If you were the staff member or a teacher who was supervising students in the cafeteria when this incident occurred, how would you have handled it?

_____

_____

2. What options are available to a teacher or staff member in a similar predicament?

_____

_____

★   ★   ★   ★   ★

This story was actually shared with me by an African American teacher after I gave a presentation at the school where this incident occurred. According to this teacher, the adult in charge of the situation chose the most extreme option. She telephoned security and the boy was arrested. At the time when I visited the school, he was still incarcerated in a juvenile detention facility.

Case Study 3 is also about an African American male student. It consists of an e-mail that an African American mother sent to me in October 2007, one day after she heard me give a keynote address about African American males at a college in New York. You'll read half of the e-mail and then respond to related questions, then read the second part and complete Exercise 6E, which I divided into two parts.

EXERCISE 6E: RESPONDING TO PART 1 OF CASE STUDY 3

Read the following case study, and answer the related questions as honestly as you can.

Part 1: An E-mail From an African American Mother

Dear Dr. Thompson:

I would like to thank you for giving a thought provoking keynote speech yesterday. As an African American mother of four African American male children, I need all the ammunition I can get to raise my children to be successful men. I have many stories to tell about my experiences with my children in the public school system, but I will only tell you one. This is why your speech hit so close to home. I will start by telling you that my youngest son is receiving special education services for being diagnosed as ADHD [attention deficit hyperactivity disorder]. If I knew then what I know now, there might not have been a story to tell. At this time, I was not giving him any prescribed drugs because deep down in my heart I knew he did not need it.

On Valentine's Day in 2006, my son at that time was 11 years old. At this time, my son was in a 12:1:1 (12 students, 1 teacher, and 1 instructional aide) class setting. My son's cell phone went off in the class (which was his fault because it should not have been on in the first place).

1. If you were the teacher in a class where an African American boy's cell phone went off in class—even though students weren't allowed to have cell phones at this school—how would you handle this situation?

     _____

     _____

2. What options are available to a teacher in a similar predicament?

     _____

     _____

Now, before you complete the second part of Exercise 6E, please read the rest of the e-mail.

Part 2: An E-mail From an African American Mother

My son went to turn it off when the teacher tried to take it from him. He would not allow her to take the cell phone so they struggled. In the struggle, she took his phone. So he took her phone and ran out the classroom. The first person he encountered was a security guard. When he explained what happened to the security guard, she advised him to call 911, which he did. When he called 911, he told the operator that the teacher touched him inappropriately.

I was called at this point and told that my son was in the office and when they had the whole story that they would call me back. When they called me back it was to tell me that my 11-year-old son was being arrested, but they could not tell me for what. I do not have to tell you I was hysterical. I immediately left my job and was there when they handcuffed my son. I must also tell you that two other Black males were also arrested and taken to the precinct with my son that day from this school. I was in shock. This was still not real to me at this time. If it was not for my boss I would not have made the right decision. He made sure I had a lawyer immediately for my son.

The next thing you know, the police showed up and my son was taken out of school in handcuffs. The teacher was fine until the police came and started questioning her. Then she claimed that he pushed her. The police claimed that I was not an involved parent and that I never returned any of the teacher's calls. I was livid at this point because I am a very involved parent. I am always active in the Parents Association and always made sure the teachers and administrators knew who I was. Then she claimed that she was not feeling good and she was taken away in an ambulance. The main reason why I was so livid is because this teacher not only knew my child before he came into her class, but her mother was the paraprofessional in my son's class the prior year and [had known] my son since he was in Pre-Kindergarten and [she knew] that I was an involved parent.

The next day was the Parents-Teachers conference. At this time, my two youngest sons were in the same school, so I went to the conference to see my sons' teachers. This is when I found out that my son's (the 11 year old) teacher was out and no one knew when she was coming back. As I was talking to the Parent Coordinator at the school, she told me the incident was in the Daily News that day. This court case went on for six months because the DA was unable to interview the teacher for four months. Luckily I had a good lawyer and an ignorant DA who the judge chastised in court for allowing this case to go on for so long without any supporting evidence. The judge ruled in my son's favor, stating if he stayed out of trouble for six months, the records would be sealed. My son was not found guilty of any crime. If this teacher cared, she would not have had my son arrested and traumatized for the rest of his life. Teachers are supposed to be trained to teach our students and look out for their best interest. There is no way that an adult with a conscience could stand by and have an 11-year-old child arrested and charged with grand larceny and filing a false report over a cell phone going off in school.

The moral of this story is that teachers (who are not African American) do not care about our African American children. The mere fact that his initial report was never addressed shows that what our males think does not matter. During this time, I felt that I had failed as a mother because I allowed this to happen. Two years later, my son is no longer in a 12:1:1 class; he is in 8th grade and doing very well and on track to go to high school next year. I decided that no matter what, I would continue to nurture, encourage, motivate, and mentor my sons to be strong African American males in a society that is constantly building obstacles for them not to succeed. I am constantly trying to re-educate myself on how to be the best mother for my children and any other child that can benefit from my guidance.

3. After the boy's cell phone went off in class, what could the teacher have done to prevent this situation from escalating to the point that it did?

_____

_____

4. According to the boy's mother, "If this teacher cared, she would not have had my son arrested and traumatized for the rest of his life. Teachers are supposed to be trained to teach our students and look out for their best interest. There is no way that an adult with a conscience could stand by and have an 11-year-old child arrested and

charged with grand larceny and filing a false report over a cell phone going off in school." Please explain why you agree or disagree with this mother's statements.

_____

_____

5. The mother also said, "The moral of this story is that teachers (who are not African American) do not care about our African American children." Explain why you agree or disagree with her statement.

_____

_____

6. What did you learn from this e-mail that can help you improve your classroom management skills?

_____

_____

★   ★   ★   ★   ★

The last case study is based on a true story that I recently read in a fascinating book that I will tell you more about after you read Case Study 4. I have divided this case study into three segments, which are followed by related exercises.

EXERCISE 6F: RESPONDING TO PART 1 OF CASE STUDY 4

Read the following case study, and answer the related question as honestly as you can.

Part 1: A Place of Torment

In the early 1960s, six-year-old Sandra, an energetic little girl, started elementary school. Like most children, she was excited. But her excitement soon turned to horror. It turned out that she was the only child in the entire school who had "brown" skin. Although her parents were white, for some unknown reason, Sandra had the appearance of being biracial: half-black and half-white. Because of her skin tone and hair texture, she was quickly ostracized by most of the children at the school. Ostracism was bad enough, but soon, the isolation turned to subtle and overt bullying. Her classmates not only called her racist names, they also stole her belongings, refused to drink from the same water fountain that she drank from, hid her school books so that she couldn't complete assignments, and harassed her in other ways. Sandra repeatedly complained to her teacher about the harassment.

1. If you were her teacher, how would you handle her complaints?

_____

_____

Part 2: A Place of Torment

Unfortunately, Sandra's teacher not only refused to take her complaints seriously, but he also often sided with her tormentors because he believed that a child who looked black or biracial did not belong at the school. During this time, Sandra developed chronic anxiety, began wetting the bed each night, and started vomiting on a regular basis. She often had difficulty concentrating on her schoolwork, and she often cried in class. After realizing that her teacher had no plans to handle the situation, Sandra began to retaliate against her tormentors. To her dismay, however, when she fought back, the teacher always punished her in such a humiliating way that she sometimes urinated on herself in class. This thrilled her tormentors.

2. Unlike the other case studies that you've read in this chapter, this story took place several decades ago, and in South Africa instead of the United States. In your opinion, how likely or unlikely is it that a similar situation could occur in the United States in current times, and why?

_____

_____

Part 3: A Place of Torment

During the four years that Sandra attended the Piet Retief Primary School in South Africa, she experienced overt racism and physical and psychological abuse from adults and students at the school. Although a few students befriended her, most of her time at the school was painful and unbearable. What she didn't know was that from the moment she arrived, adults at the school had started conspiring to have her removed on the grounds that even though she was legally "white," her biracial appearance meant that she didn't belong at the school. Four years later, she was kicked out of the school after being officially designated as "colored," and her case became one of the most famous in South African history. I hope that you will read Judith Stone's powerful biography of Sandra Laing because the book, _When She Was White: The True Story of a Family Divided by Race_, contains many important lessons about race relations, racism, and how mental baggage can impede your progress with students of color, especially black and biracial students.[13]

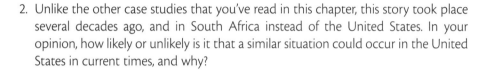

The final exercise of this chapter requires you to synthesize what you have learned about yourself and classroom management.

EXERCISE 6G: REFLECTING ON WHAT YOU HAVE LEARNED

Please respond to each question or statement as honestly as you can.

1. Now that you have read the entire chapter, how confident are you about your classroom management skills, and why?

_____

_____

2. What did you learn about the importance of not letting minor situations escalate?

_____

_____

3. What did you learn about the importance of taking students' complaints about bullying seriously?

_____

_____

4. How will you ensure that African American students are treated fairly in your classroom?

_____

_____

5. What steps will you take in order to continue to improve your classroom management skills?

_____

_____

★ ★ ★ ★ ★

GROUP ACTIVITY FOR PROFESSIONAL DEVELOPMENT AND COURSE WORK

1. As a group, engage in role playing by having one member act as the teacher, several members pretend to be misbehaving students, several members pretend to be well-behaved students, and the other members serve as observers and recorders who will take notes about what transpires.

   For example, one misbehaving student can be an excessive talker. Another can interrupt the teacher repeatedly by insisting on being allowed to leave the classroom for a drink of water, to run an errand, and so on. Another can pretend to take a nap, and another can pass notes to other students. The teacher should write a lesson plan on the board, try to implement the lesson plan, and try to get all students to cooperate.

2. After about 15 minutes, the recorders can share their observations, and the entire group can discuss what happened and how teachers can handle similar situations.

7

Using Wisdom in Assessing Students in Spite of the High-Stakes-Testing Mania

Testing is an important part of teaching. Students are required to take many quizzes and tests on the information that their teachers have taught, and they are also required to take standardized tests. College-bound students must take additional tests as well. I included a "testing" chapter in this book because, historically, African American students have had lower average standardized test scores than many of their nonblack peers. Therefore, improving African American students' test scores has become a top priority for school administrators and teachers—and also a source of great frustration for many. So in this chapter, I share research and strategies about how you can improve African American students' test scores. I'll also ask you to complete several related exercises, starting with Exercise 7A.

EXERCISE 7A: EXAMINING YOUR VIEWS ABOUT STANDARDIZED TESTS

Please respond to each question as honestly as possible.

1. When you were a K–12 student, how did you feel about having to take tests and quizzes?

   _____

   _____

2. What type of grades did you usually earn on tests and quizzes?

   _____

   _____

3. During your K–12 education, how did you feel about having to take standardized tests?

   _____

   _____

4. As an educator, how do you feel about being required to give standardized tests to your students?

   _____

   _____

5. How can you use students' test scores to help students?

   _____

   _____

6. How can you use test scores to harm your students?

   _____

   _____

7. How can you use test scores to improve your teaching?

   _____

   _____

8. Review your answers to the previous questions and explain what they reveal about your views on testing.

   _____

   _____

★   ★   ★   ★   ★

EDUCATORS' VIEWS
ABOUT STANDARDIZED TESTS

Several researchers have done what I did in the previous exercise: asked teachers how they feel about standardized tests. For example, in "Test Your Attitude," an article that was published in *Scholastic*, Kathe Taylor and Sherry Walton wrote that many teachers have negative attitudes about standardized tests and may not realize that their attitudes impact their students in negative ways. According to these authors, teachers' "words may encourage children to do their best, but our tone of voice and our facial expressions may betray us."[1] In another study, researchers at the University of Connecticut concluded that "teachers and students feel a tremendous amount of pressure . . . to produce high student test scores." This pressure has a negative effect on how and what teachers teach, and teachers in underperforming schools are affected more adversely than other teachers.[2] The National Center for Education Statistics "Schools and Staffing Survey (SASS)" also revealed that many teachers are very concerned about standardized tests. During the 2004–2005 school year, for example, approximately 40% of the public school teachers who participated in the study said, "I worry about the security of my job because of the performance of my students on state and/or local tests."[3] In my case, during one of the workshops that I conducted, I asked the participants to respond to a questionnaire about testing. Fifty-eight percent said that in their opinion, K–12 students are required to take too many tests, and 17% said that students should be required to take fewer tests. (See Appendix J for more information.)

STUDENTS' VIEWS ABOUT STANDARDIZED TESTS

Just as teachers have strong, and often negative, views about standardized tests, so too do students. As I mentioned in the previous section, the researchers at the University of Connecticut found that pressures related to standardized tests adversely affected teachers and students. One result is that students end up getting a "drill and practice type of curriculum and instruction."[4] This pressure can even affect gifted students negatively and cause them to become frustrated, resentful, and disengaged.[5]

In the study that I conducted at an underperforming high school and described in *Up Where We Belong*, I wanted to know how students felt about standardized tests. I learned that many students said that they didn't take the tests seriously and that many believed that their teachers didn't take the tests seriously, that their teachers were failing to adequately prepare them for the standardized tests, that the tests were a waste of time, and that many saw no benefit to doing well on the tests. Black and Latino students were more likely to say that the tests were a waste of time, and they were less likely than whites to say that passing standardized tests was important to them. Furthermore, black students were less likely than whites and Latinos to say that most of their teachers had done a good job of preparing them for the standardized tests.[6]

HOW TEACHERS CAN IMPROVE AFRICAN AMERICAN STUDENTS' TEST SCORES

Regardless of how you feel about standardized tests, and regardless of how students feel about them, the fact remains that standardized tests are required by most K–12 public schools. In other words, educators and students are stuck with them. Therefore, as an educator, it is in your best interest to know how to increase your students' chances of doing well on standardized tests. Because African American students tend to have lower standardized test scores than other students, knowing how to help them do well on standardized tests should be an important component of your quest to increase your efficacy with them. Therefore, in the next section, we'll look at specific strategies, starting with Exercise 7B.

EXERCISE 7B: IDENTIFYING THE STRATEGIES THAT YOU KNOW

Please respond to each question as honestly as possible.

1. When you were a K–12 student, how much time did most of your teachers spend preparing you for standardized tests?

   _____

   _____

2. What were the best strategies that your K–12 teachers used to prepare you for standardized tests?

   _____

   _____

3. What were the least effective strategies that your K–12 teachers used to prepare you for standardized tests?

   _____

   _____

4. Review the following list of test preparation strategies. Circle the strategies that you have used to help your own students prepare for standardized tests or that you believe are the most useful strategies to help students prepare for standardized tests.

Test Preparation Strategies

Model test-taking strategies

Give practice tests

Tie the curriculum to the information on which students will be tested

Teach students how to read test questions

Teach students how to select the best choice

Offer tutoring

Build students' confidence

Spend enough time on skill development

Teach students how to identify key words

Familiarize yourself with the test format

Reteach information

Focus on areas of weakness

Teach lessons in the test format

Teach concepts

Review information

Explain why the test is important

Use visuals

Use hands-on activities

Cover the test objectives

Assess students at the beginning of the year

Devote enough time to test preparation

Use mnemonic devices

Give examples and sample questions

Teach students how to pace themselves

Help students deal with test anxiety

Encourage students to get enough sleep

Encourage students to eat breakfast

5. Please review the list again. Which strategies do you think are the least effective in helping students prepare for standardized tests?

_____

_____

STRATEGIES THAT EDUCATORS RECOMMEND

The list of test preparation strategies that you just examined actually came from the "Test" questionnaire that I administered to workshop participants a few years ago (see Appendix J). They were asked to "list five strategies that teachers can use to prepare students for standardized tests." The items on the list are listed in order, with the most frequently cited strategies first and the least frequently cited strategies last. The five most frequently cited strategies were as follows:

- Model test-taking strategies (60%)
- Give practice tests (48%)
- Tie the curriculum to the information on which students will be tested (37%)
- Teach students how to read test questions (33%)
- Teach students how to select the best choice (22%)

Which of these five were also strategies that you circled and consider to be effective? Which, in your opinion, should not be on the list of the top five?

STRATEGIES THAT EDUCATORS
APPEAR TO BE LESS LIKELY TO USE

The least-cited recommendations from the workshop participants were very interesting. They were as follows:

- Cover test objectives (6%)
- Assess students at the beginning of the year (6%)
- Devote enough time to test preparation (6%)
- Use mnemonic devices (5%)

- Give examples and sample questions (5%)
- Teach students how to pace themselves (5%)
- Help students deal with test anxiety (3%)
- Encourage students to get enough sleep (3%)
- Encourage students to eat breakfast (3%)

Which, if any, of the above strategies do you believe are important and should have been cited by more of the workshop participants?

I hope that you were troubled by at least three of the least frequently cited strategies, especially when it comes to preparing African American students for standardized tests. Those three strategies are "assess students at the beginning of the year," "devote enough time to test preparation," and "help students deal with test anxiety."

Early Assessment

Assessing students at the beginning of the year is important so that you can uncover students' areas of strength and weakness. So often, African American students struggle with algebra and other types of mathematics because teachers don't realize that the students are lacking one or more basic prerequisite math skills. Doing reading and writing assessments at the beginning of the year can also give you crucial information about students' skills that can help you tailor lesson plans in order to address their academic weaknesses. In other words, this is not merely a good strategy to prepare students for standardized tests, but a good teaching strategy in general.

Test Preparation

It seems obvious to me that in order to adequately prepare students for standardized tests, teachers should make sure that they are devoting enough time to test preparation. However, often, this isn't what happens. As I stated previously, the black students who participated in the study on which *Up Where We Belong* is based were less likely than whites and Latinos to say that most of their teachers had done a good job of preparing them for standardized tests. Spending enough time preparing students for standardized tests requires you to find ways to link lesson plans to the tests by emphasizing skills and information on which students will be tested. Another complaint from students who participated in the *Up Where We Belong* study was that the curriculum in most of their classes was not connected to the information that they were expected to know for the standardized tests. Dr. Claude Steele, an expert on standardized tests, said that the type of schools that students attend and the ways in which they are taught can affect their performance on standardized tests.[7]

Test Anxiety

Helping students deal with test anxiety is also crucial for teachers who want to improve the standardized test scores of African American students.[8] Many students, not just African Americans, suffer from test anxiety. When people feel anxious, they are less likely to perform at their best. Students who have had a history of doing poorly on tests may become so anxious at the thought of having to take another test that they may actually fail the test or refuse to even try.[9] Stereotype threat can affect any student—regardless of race—but many African American students are aware that they are not expected to perform well on tests as a result of stereotype threat.

According to Dr. Joshua Aronson, *stereotype threat* is "apprehension arising from the awareness of a negative stereotype or personal reputation in a situation where the stereotype is relevant, and thus confirmable."[10] Dr. Steele said that stereotype threat tends to affect high achievers more than low achievers, that it can raise a student's blood pressure, and that it can be "distracting enough, upsetting enough, to undermine a person's performance right in the middle of a test."[11] In fact, some very brilliant people have suffered from test anxiety. One example is my late sister Tammie, who was studying for the bar exam at the time of her death, in 1995.[12] Another example is Gregor Mendel, whose extreme anxiety not only caused him to become bedridden at times, but also caused him to twice fail the exam that he needed to pass in order to become a teacher. He not only became a famous scientist, but today, Mendel is known as "the Father of Genetics."[13]

One solution, according to Steele, is for educators to "create learning situations, schooling situations, where people can feel secure."[14] Aronson said that educators can reduce the effects of stereotype threat by reducing fear, emphasizing to students that intelligence is not fixed, teaching them about misconceptions related to intelligence, and teaching students about stereotype threat and ways to deal with anxiety.[15]

A SUMMARY OF KEY POINTS TO REMEMBER ABOUT PREPARING AFRICAN AMERICAN STUDENTS FOR STANDARDIZED TESTS

There are several main points that I would like you to remember about preparing African American K–12 students for standardized tests. In the next section, I explain these points.

1. Don't Give Mixed Messages

Remember that your attitude can affect students' attitudes about standardized tests. If you don't like giving the tests (and who really does?), you can unknowingly convey that message to students and impact their performance. In "Test Your Attitude," an article by Kathe Taylor and Sherry Walton, the authors said, "Ideally, we should entice children into viewing tests as an interesting and manageable challenge. . . ." but before teachers can do this, they must get rid of their own baggage.[16] Dealing with all types of mental baggage that can impede your progress with African American students has been a recurring theme in this book. Dealing with your baggage about testing is another way to increase your efficacy. In fact, according to Taylor and Walton, "Becoming aware of your negative emotions about testing is the first step toward getting them under control, making you even more effective at helping your students tackle tests."[17]

2. Devote Enough Time to Test Preparation

Obviously, one of the single most effective strategies that educators can use to prepare African American students for standardized tests is to make sure that they are devoting enough time to test preparation. In my opinion, instead of spending a week or two preparing students before you are scheduled to give a test, it is important to teach test-taking strategies *throughout* the school year. The best way to do this is to tie daily lesson plans to state standards, to give lots of practice tests, and to make sure that students

- understand the main types of tests (multiple choice, true–false, essay, fill-in-the-blank, etc.),
- know how to find the main idea or main point,[18]
- know problem-solving skills that include understanding the task that they are asked to perform,[19]
- understand the importance of reading directions carefully,[20]
- can solve word problems and other important math tasks,[21]
- know how to use a process of elimination in order to eliminate wrong answers,[22] and
- have good reading comprehension skills that include knowing how to differentiate between fact and opinion, drawing conclusions, making predictions, and making inferences.[23]

3. Explain the Short-Term and Long-Term Benefits of Doing Well on Standardized Tests

African American students also need to know why the standardized tests are important. An African American male high school student who participated in the *Up Where We Belong* study said that in the past, he hadn't been serious about doing well on standardized tests. According to this student, "It don't count for our grades, and they give us twenty tests a year. It don't make no sense to give us all these tests. If they don't count, why take your time on it?"[24] His attitude was similar to that of other students who participated in the study. You can solve this dilemma by making sure that your students understand both why they are required to take standardized tests and the short-term and long-term benefits of doing well on the tests.

4. Help Students Deal With Test Anxiety

In "Reducing Test Anxiety," Professor Joe Martin gave advice to a college student with test anxiety. One of the strategies that he shared is something that teachers should emphasize to African American students: "The best way to relieve stress in any situation is to keep the task or problem in perspective. . . . It's okay to take tests seriously . . . but not too seriously!"[25] This is good advice for you to remember and good advice to share with students. While you want all of your students to do their very best on the tests, and while you want to spend an adequate amount of time preparing them to do well, the test is not so important that it determines either their self-worth or yours as an educator. Therefore, an obvious way that you can reduce test anxiety is to emphasize to students that even though doing well on the test is important, the test is merely one way of determining how much students know. It cannot tell everything about how knowledgeable they are about the test subject matter.

5. Keep in Mind That the Test Doesn't Tell the Whole Story

In order to get rid of your mental baggage about standardized tests and do a good job of preparing African American students for standardized tests, you should also understand the following points:

- All standardized tests contain measurement flaws.[26]
- Many standardized tests actually measure students' socioeconomic status rather than what they have been taught in class.[27]
- Middle-class and upper-class students are more likely than low-income students to have been exposed to the information on standardized tests outside of class.[28]
- The tests have a very racist history. Here are some related quotes from Dr. Steele, a test expert and professor at Stanford University:

> The area of standardized testing and intelligence testing has always been one of the most controversial areas of psychology. . . . It has often been used as a way of implementing racist intent, most recently with regard to Blacks. . . . But in the post-World War I wave of immigration it was used to screen out Southern Europeans, Jews, and other groups who did not score well on tests at that particular time. So it has, as a tool, a very, very racist past.[29]
>
> All kinds of things can contribute to performance and it muddles up the diagnosticity of the test. . . . The SAT and no standardized test is that kind [of] measure [that] can bear the burden of

fairly assessing academic potential for all groups in society or all people for that matter in society. We just don't have that.[30]

6. Become Familiar With the Qualities of Effective Teachers

In a previous chapter, I mentioned that according to African American students, outstanding teachers make the curriculum interesting, comprehensible, and relevant. Outstanding teachers are also willing to give extra help to struggling students, and they are fair and patient. Researchers at the North Central Regional Educational Laboratory have synthesized the research on teacher effectiveness and compiled a list that contains great information for teachers. Many of the findings are points that I've covered in previous chapters. According to these researchers, effective teachers

- have good classroom management skills and the class climate is orderly, so that students can learn;
- review important subject matter on a daily basis;
- use diverse teaching strategies;
- work with small groups;
- give students feedback about their progress on a regular basis;
- stay in touch with parents;
- "adjust the difficulty level of the material to student ability";
- "pace the amount of information presented to the class"; and
- "check student progress continually by asking questions of all students, and relate new learning to prior learning."[31]

EXERCISE 7C: REFLECTING ON WHAT YOU HAVE LEARNED ABOUT TESTING

Please respond to each question as honestly as possible.

1. What are the three main points that you would like to remember about preparing African American students for standardized tests?

_____

_____

_____

2. What strategies do you plan to use to prepare African American students for standardized tests?

_____

_____

★   ★   ★   ★   ★

GROUP ACTIVITY FOR PROFESSIONAL DEVELOPMENT AND COURSE WORK

1. As a group, examine African American students' standardized test scores for local K–12 schools by accessing the information from your state's Department of Education Web site. For example, two or three small groups can examine the scores for the elementary schools in the district; another group can look at middle school scores, and a third group can look at high school scores.

2. Each small group can analyze the information and create a report that includes recommendations to be shared with the larger group.

3. The larger group can determine what the scores reveal about the school district.

4. By synthesizing the recommendations from each small group, the larger group can create an action plan that can be shared with district officials in the form of a short report or through some other medium.

8

Learning From Classroom Scenarios and Other Problems That Concern Educators

By now, you should know a lot of information about how you can become a more effective educator of African American students. You have read stories, research, and strategies about many topics that we will return to in this chapter. Moreover, in this chapter, you will have a chance to identify the areas that you feel most confident about and the ones that you feel you still need growth in, and more important, you will have opportunities to put yourself in the role of a mentor or expert educator. Each section begins with an exercise that is related to one of the main topics that we covered in previous chapters. Next, you will read related case studies, questions, and stories that were shared with me by other educators and use the information that you've learned to solve these dilemmas. Finally, you'll be able to compare your solutions to the ones that I offer.

IDENTIFYING THE PERSONAL BENEFITS OF INCREASING ONE'S EFFICACY WITH AFRICAN AMERICAN K–12 STUDENTS

EXERCISE 8A: REMEMBERING THE PERSONAL BENEFITS OF INCREASING ONE'S EFFICACY WITH AFRICAN AMERICAN STUDENTS

Please respond to each question as honestly as possible.

1. Based on everything that you have read in this book so far, what, in your opinion, are the main ways that you will personally benefit from increasing your efficacy with African American students?

   _____

   _____

2. In what way, if any, has your response to the aforementioned question changed since you first answered it in Chapter 1?

   _____

   _____

3. How confident are you about your ability to persuade other educators that there are personal benefits to increasing their efficacy with African American students, and why do you feel this way?

   _____

   _____

★   ★   ★   ★   ★

You are about to read and respond to a question that a first-year teacher included in a letter that she wrote to me after she and her classmates were required to read *Through Ebony Eyes* in a teacher education course in which they were enrolled.

CASE STUDY 1: HELPABLE VERSUS NON-HELPABLE STUDENTS

"How can you distinguish a 'helpable' student from a 'non-helpable' student? As a novice teacher, my naïve goal is to change every student I come in contact with. However, I realize that reality is that not every student will be reachable. . . . I would like to know at what point do you realize that the student is adamant about not being helped?"

1. How would you respond to this question if a first-year teacher at your school came to you for advice?

_____

_____

2. Do you believe that there are helpable and non-helpable students? If so, what are the differences between the two groups, and how can you determine which students fall into which group?

_____

_____

CASE STUDY 2

A middle-aged white woman wrote the following comment on a questionnaire that I distributed at one of my workshops for educators:

> "My concern is that I know I may have helped a lot of students but I may have affected several of them without knowing."

1. What would you tell her if she were one of your colleagues?

_____

_____

REVISITING CASE STUDIES 1 AND 2

Both of the previous case studies are related to Chapter 1 of this book because they are directly and indirectly related to the importance of helping educators understand the personal benefits of increasing their efficacy with African American students. In fact, one way to address both scenarios would be to share the personal benefits that you identified for yourself with both of these teachers and then help them to identify how they would personally benefit from continuing to do their best with all students.

More than that, both case studies are related to the main job of educators: to educate *all* students to the best of their ability. In other words, even though many students may appear to be apathetic, unmotivated, and even resistant to what the teacher is trying to do, it is still the teacher's job to do his or her best to ensure that every student has the opportunity to receive outstanding instruction and an empowering curriculum.

In terms of whether or not certain students are helpable or not, I will repeat what I've said in previous articles and books that I've written: "Educators shouldn't play God with other people's children." It is not the teacher's job to sort students into categories as if teachers are the ultimate masters of students' fates. It is the teacher's job to do his or her best. Moreover, as I revealed in a previous chapter, most of my elementary school teachers viewed me as a failure who had little or no academic potential. Obviously, they were wrong. Therefore, it is very important for you to keep in mind that you should never give up on any student, nor condone the behaviors and attitudes of colleagues who do. After all, you are being paid to educate all of the students in your classes.

Case Study 2 is another reminder that, as educators, sometimes we won't know the outcome of our hard work. An older teacher appeared to be unsure about whether or not her work was having a positive impact on her students. In cases where students have been subjected to low expectations, poor teaching, and other forms of inequality of educational opportunity before they finally get a good teacher, it might take a long time for those students to make the academic progress that a teacher might hope to see or that will be reflected by higher standardized test scores. For example, if a seventh grader is reading at the third-grade level at the beginning of the school year and is reading at the fifth-grade level by the end of the school year, that student made progress that might not necessarily show up on a standardized test—but the student made progress nonetheless. Also, it is very common for good teachers to work extremely hard to try to reach underperforming students or students from challenging backgrounds and to never find out how the students ultimately turned out. My own more than 30-year quest to find Mrs. Tessem, my sixth-grade teacher, is a good example of this. For decades, she never knew how well the time and energy that she invested in me had paid off. Furthermore, remember that the resiliency research indicates that most students from challenging backgrounds do turn out well as adults.

Therefore, both of these case studies should remind us of the importance of focusing on the aspects of students' lives that we can change and of constantly reminding ourselves and others of the personal benefits that we receive for choosing to become outstanding educators of African Americans and other students.

EXERCISE 8B: REMEMBERING THAT NEGATIVE MINDSETS CAN UNDERMINE YOUR WORK WITH AFRICAN AMERICAN STUDENTS

Please respond to each question as honestly as possible.

1. Based on everything that you have read in this book so far, how can negative mindsets and stereotypes impede your work with African American students?

_____

_____

2. In what ways, if any, have your views about African American K–12 students changed since you began reading this book?

_____

_____

3. How confident are you about your ability to persuade other educators that their own mental baggage can prevent them from working effectively with African American students, and why do you feel this way?

_____

_____

★ ★ ★ ★ ★

Now, I'd like you to read Case Studies 3 and 4, which are about mental baggage, and answer the related questions.

CASE STUDY 3: HOW CAN I HELP OTHER TEACHERS?

In a letter that she sent to me after reading *Through Ebony Eyes*, a female teacher at a predominantly Latino school wrote:

> As a Latina myself, I have experienced many of the adversities that African Americans also encountered and continue to encounter in education. What I can definitely agree with as both a student who experienced this, and now as a teacher who works with culturally insensitive and uninformed educators, is even today, teachers genuinely believe that Latinos and African Americans are culturally and genetically inferior.
>
> I teach at a predominately Latino school and often find myself having to defend students' potential for learning. I really feel that recent contributions to the field and to a select group of the population like African Americans and Latinos will make a difference in the perceptions that teachers have of students.
>
> My question now, however, is "How can I most effectively transform the erroneous perceptions that teachers today have of students?" Many will continue teaching for another twenty or thirty years. "How can we [change] this negative outlook for the future leaders of America?"

1. According to this teacher, some of her colleagues are "culturally insensitive" and "uninformed" about Latino and African American students. Explain why you believe that this is a widespread

problem or a problem that is merely isolated to a few teachers at a few schools.

_____

_____

2. This teacher also said that "... even today, teachers genuinely believe that Latinos and African Americans are culturally and genetically inferior." Explain why you agree or disagree with her statement.

_____

_____

3. If this teacher came to you and asked, "How can I most effectively transform the erroneous perceptions that teachers today have of students?" what would you tell her, and why?

_____

_____

CASE STUDY 4: MY PROBLEMATIC MINDSETS

On the "Searching for Solutions" questionnaire that I distributed to educators who attended a workshop I conducted at a high school, a Chinese American school employee who was in the 20–29 years-old age range asked the following simple question:

"How do I deal with my own problematic mindsets or stereotypes toward African American students once I admit it?"

1. If this woman were one of your coworkers who came to you for advice, what would you tell her?

_____

_____

REVISITING CASE STUDIES 3 AND 4

In my opinion, Case Study 4 is much easier to address than Case Study 3. The best way to respond to a coworker's question of "How do I deal with my own problematic mindsets or stereotypes toward African American students once I admit it?" is twofold. First, she deserves a commendation for her honesty. It takes a lot of courage to admit what she acknowledged in a society where most people remain in denial or are too afraid to admit that they harbor mental baggage about African Americans and other groups. Next, it would be helpful to share with her some of the information that you learned in Chapter 2 of this book and review some of the cognitive restructuring strategies with her. Suggesting that she keep a journal to record her thoughts and interactions with African Americans over a 21-day period, that she monitor her thoughts during this time, and that she critique her negative thoughts after they occur are a few of the recommendations that you can make. You can also suggest that she read some of the books and articles that I have recommended to you. You could go a step further by giving or loaning some of this reading material to her and meeting her for lunch periodically to discuss the books and articles. This might be a great way to help you review some of the information that you already know and, at the same time, help you provide a safe environment for a colleague to discuss sensitive subject matter. But more important, by choosing to help this colleague in any way that you can, you will be helping every single African American student who might be treated more humanely by her as a result of the assistance that you gave to her.

For Case Study 3, there are several ways that you could approach this situation if the aforementioned Latina teacher were one of your colleagues who came to you for help. First, you could blow her off by making it clear to her that you didn't want to be bothered with her concerns. This is often a tactic used by individuals who actually have the same mental baggage that she was complaining about. In other words, these types of teachers actually believe that African American and Latino students are genetically and culturally inferior, but because it's not politically correct to articulate these beliefs in many settings, they won't tell her the true reason why they won't address her concerns.

A second option is that you could warn this new teacher that she's treading on dangerous ground. Because she's new and probationary, her job might be jeopardized if she ruffles the wrong feathers. Some, seemingly well meaning, veteran teachers use this approach with new teachers in order to silence them and instill fear in them about verbalizing their concerns about controversial issues.

Third, you could tell her that you are sorry that she feels this way but you don't really know what you can do to help. This might indicate that you don't feel confident about your ability to give advice about the topics that concern her, you don't want to "go there" and possibly say anything that might come back to haunt you, or it might mean that you genuinely don't know how to help her.

A fourth option is to do your best to address her concerns—even if you don't have all of the answers, and even if you aren't sure of what to say. If you don't know what to say in response to her questions, a logical solution would be to be honest. Saying, "I'm not sure how you can change other teachers' perceptions of African American and Latino students," is not only an acceptable response, but it's a way to enter into a mutually beneficial dialogue with this teacher. This dialogue could lead to ongoing discussions about alternatives that she might consider, and possibly even a friendship.

Another option is that you can become proactive. Even if you haven't seen or heard evidence at your school to corroborate her concerns, you can ask her why she believes what she does, offer to help, and work with her and school administrators to find ways to improve the school climate through professional development activities for all of the adults at the school site.

The bottom line is that if one teacher perceives that her colleagues have negative mental baggage about any group of students, this perception can affect teacher morale, student morale, and the entire school climate; it can create a host of problems that will prevent teachers from working effectively and students from receiving a quality education. Therefore, in my opinion, it would be in your best interest to take the proactive approach.

EXERCISE 8C: REMEMBERING WHY THE TOPIC OF RACISM CAN'T BE IGNORED

Please respond to each question as honestly as possible.

1. Based on everything that you have read in this book so far, explain how racism affects the school-related experiences of African American K–12 students.

   _____

   _____

2. How confident are you about your ability to discuss racism and racial issues with your students, and why?

   _____

   _____

3. How confident are you about your ability to give advice to a colleague who requests your help in dealing with a racial problem, and why?

   _____

   _____

★ ★ ★ ★ ★

Throughout the years, I have received more letters and e-mails that deal with racism and racial issues than any other topic. Furthermore, many of the workshop participants who completed the questionnaires that I have described to you in this book wrote questions about racial issues. Consequently, it was difficult for me to decide which case studies to include in the next section, but I tried to include the ones that I thought would be the most helpful to your professional growth in terms of helping you increase your efficacy with African American students. As you've already done throughout this chapter, please read each case study and answer the related question(s).

CASE STUDY 5: DIFFUSING RACIAL TENSION IN THE CLASSROOM

Here's an excerpt from a letter that a Latino teacher sent to me. At the time, he was a new teacher in a southern California city that has a history of racial strife between Latinos and African Americans.

> In my experience with students from challenging backgrounds, I am frequently working with a majority of Latino youth, as well as a small population of African American youth. For the most part, the two groups of students get along well, yet from time to time, there are some Latino youth who cause racial conflicts against their fellow African American students. In fact, the city where I work and live in has a Latino gang that prides itself in espousing racist attitudes toward African Americans.
>
> My approach has always been zero tolerance of any racial slurs and or gestures that can lead toward physical violence. . . . As a Latino male, I have in the past lost popularity and influence with some of the Latino students over the course of action I take against ethnic intolerance. In the end, however, I believe students see my non-biased approach as the right choice, which allows me to continue working with them in a constructive manner. Nevertheless, what advice might you give to [me so that I can] diffuse ethnic tension between minority students?

1. If this teacher came to you for advice about ways to diffuse tension among students from different racial or ethnic groups, what would you tell him, and why?

   _____

   _____

CASE STUDY 6: FEELING "SHUT-DOWN" AND FRUSTRATED

The following excerpt is from a letter that a white teacher sent to me after he read *Through Ebony Eyes:*

I am confronted by people I considered open-minded who seem to think I'm too sensitive, too analytical, or that I read too much into things. If I say that the reason why contemporary racism is so dangerous is precisely because it's indirect or hidden in institutional policies, I'm treated as though I don't have proof to back up my argument, and [I'm] just an emotional liberal. I wind up feeling shut-down and frustrated because most people, myself included, don't fully understand how complicated these issues really are.

Specifically, I identified with the section on White teachers feeling as though they didn't have a chance in the classroom. My fear is that my students will immediately write me off as having nothing to offer them because of past negative experiences with White teachers, and I won't be able to form relationships with them. I know that all I can ask of myself is to do my best, but I also know that good intentions are not enough.

I've often felt frustrated when confronting issues of race because of the "color-blind" idea, but I know that anyone who thinks race isn't an issue is seeing the world through rose-colored glasses. How can I get my students to see that as a social reality our differences matter, but at the same time value each other equally?

1. If this teacher confided in you that he was fearful of being rejected by African American students merely because he is white, what would you tell him?

   _____

   _____

2. What would you tell this teacher regarding his frustration over the way that adults react to his views about institutional racism?

   _____

   _____

CASE STUDY 7: BEING ACCUSED OF RACISM

The next three questions are very similar to several others that educators wrote on the "Searching for Solutions" questionnaire.

"How do you address a student that claims you're racist because you care and don't inflate his or her grade?" (This was from a Japanese American woman who was in the 20- to 29-year-old age range.)

"How do I articulate high standards without being seen as picking on kids?" (This came from a white woman who was in the 50-plus age category.)

"How do you cope with your high standards being interpreted as racism?"(This came from a white female in the 40- to 49-year-old age range.)

1. What would you tell these teachers if they came to you for advice?

_____

_____

CASE STUDY 8: CONFUSED

Several teachers who completed the "Searching for Solutions" questionnaire also wrote questions that indicated that they weren't sure about whether or not they were really racist or whether or not they engaged in behaviors that could be viewed as racist. For example, a middle-aged white teacher asked the following:

"How do I communicate more effectively, so as not to intimidate, put down, etc., but rather relate in a way they get?"

1. What would you tell this teacher if she came to you for advice?

_____

_____

A Latina teacher in the 30- to 39-year-old age group simply asked, "Am I a racist?"

1. What would you say to her if she asked you this question?

_____

_____

A white teacher asked, "Do I portray negative vibes?"

1. What would you say to her if she asked you this question?

_____

_____

REVISITING CASE STUDIES 5 THROUGH 8

I hope that you had a lot of fun responding to Case Studies 5 through 8. I also hope that you realize that during your career as an educator, it is very likely that you will be asked to address one or more of these questions.

Let's begin by revisiting Case Study 5, which involved the Latino teacher who felt that some of his Latino students didn't like the way that he handled racial conflicts and wanted advice about how to do a better job of diffusing racial tension between African American and Latino students.

First of all, this teacher definitely deserves a commendation for his courage in doing the right thing even though it might not have allowed him to win a popularity contest with some of his students. If this teacher came to me for advice, I would applaud him and remind him that his behavior is very important because all students, even the seemingly worst-behaving students, expect the teacher to behave as the authority figure in the classroom. In order to gain respect, he has a professional and even moral obligation to set the appropriate tone in the classroom, to eradicate inappropriate behavior, and to create a classroom environment where all students feel safe and are able to perform at their optimum. Because children and adolescents are impressionable and are still in the process of developing moral and intellectual skills, it is all the more important for the teacher to set the right tone and model fairness. Apparently, this teacher was doing this well.

In terms of how to diffuse racial tension among students, I would give the same advice to the Latino teacher in Case Study 5 that I would give to the white male teacher in Case Study 6: Use the curriculum! I would advise both of these teachers to incorporate lesson plans about social justice, racism, and so on, and assign related activities, such as writing assignments, group and individualized projects, debates, whole group and small group discussions, mock trials, and so on, into the curriculum on an ongoing basis. When students are allowed to talk about real-life issues and current events taking place in their communities, in the cities in which they live, in the nation, and in the world in a safe environment, they are more likely to get along in class and work together as a community of learners. I learned this during my own years as a K–12 teacher, while teaching at a predominantly Latino high school, and many of the strategies that I described in *Through Ebony Eyes* and *Up Where We Belong* are actually strategies that I used.

The white male teacher in Case Study 6 also had another issue. He felt frustrated, shut out, and mislabeled by people—possibly colleagues—who viewed him as an idealistic liberal. If he came to me for advice, I would tell him that just because his views are unpopular among some people, doesn't mean that he's wrong. Hitler and other despots throughout history had huge followings at one point or another, but time has shown that these men and their ideas were wrong and destructive. Conversely, like prophets and Cassandra in Greek mythology, often the truth-teller is disparaged, disbelieved, and sometimes even penalized for holding unpopular views! The same is true when it comes to race relations. Some people would still prefer to destroy the messenger—if not physically, as with the murders of Dr. Martin Luther King Jr. and Medgar Evers—at least mentally. The white male teacher was being subjected to what I'd refer to as "psychological warfare" by individuals who wanted to silence and marginalize him. If he came to me for advice, I would inform him of this. I would also share some of my own related experiences with him, such as the numerous times when I have had to deal with hostile educators who didn't want to hear what I had to say about African American parents or African American students. Furthermore, I'd suggest that he read books about courageous whites who have had similar experiences. My suggestions would include the following books:

- *We Can't Teach What We Don't Know,* by Gary Howard
- *White Teachers/Diverse Classrooms,* by Julie Landsman and Chance Lewis
- *Growing Up White: A Veteran Teacher Reflects on Racism,* by Julie Landsman
- *Death at an Early Age,* by Jonathan Kozol
- *White Boy: A Memoir,* by Mark Naison
- *White Like Me: Reflecting on Race From a Privileged Son,* by Tim Wise

Case Studies 7 and 8 consist of several questions. One teacher asked "Am I racist?" First, I would commend her for having the courage to even ask a question that terrifies so many. Next, I would ask her how she herself would answer that question. Then, I would share the definition of *racist* with her and ask her if she felt that the definition fit her. Finally, I would share with her some of the strategies that I explained in Chapters 2 and 3 and suggest that she consider journaling, using the cognitive restructuring strategies, and monitoring her behavior toward African Americans. This is also what I would recommend to the teacher who wanted to communicate more effectively with African American students and to the teacher who wanted to know if she was sending off negative vibes. But the main thing that I would tell all three teachers is the importance of remembering to view and treat African American students in the same manner that they would want their own children's teachers to treat their children and also remembering to treat African American students in the way that they would have wanted their own teachers to treat them. In other words, I would paraphrase the golden rule.

EXERCISE 8D: REMEMBERING WHAT YOU'VE LEARNED ABOUT AFRICAN AMERICAN PARENTS

Please respond to each question as honestly as possible.

1. At this point, how confident are you about your ability to work with the parents and guardians of African American K–12 students, and why?

_____

_____

2. How confident are you about your ability to advise a colleague about how he or she could improve his or her relations with African American parents, and why?

_____

_____

The following case studies will give you opportunities to apply the information that you have learned about African American parents and how you can improve your relations with them. The first is based on an excerpt from a letter that an elementary school teacher sent to me after reading *Through Ebony Eyes*:

CASE STUDY 9: AN ANGRY TEACHER

It wasn't until I found myself intimately involved in the ordeals and challenges faced by teachers teaching students of color and in underprivileged communities that I was finally faced with the reality. I felt angry, cynical, and frustrated by the challenges I faced, and the lack of resources and support I received in the district where I taught. I was also angered by the lack of parental involvement despite my best efforts (home visits, phone calls, letters home, etc.).

It seemed like parents really didn't care about their children and the few who did were far and few between. I was well aware that many parents were unable to come to school because they worked constantly to make ends meet, and I made efforts to involve them in other ways and keep them informed. The parents that most frustrated me were the ones who were uninvolved for no other reason than they seemingly didn't care or didn't even bother to register their children for school. . . .

My anger was directed not only toward the district and people who didn't care enough to make their children's education meaningful, but also toward myself because I felt ineffectual and helpless in a larger system that did nothing but issue standardized tests that set children and schools up to fail.

1. This teacher didn't ask a question, but her anger and frustration about several problems, including what she perceived to be a lack of parent involvement, were quite evident. In your opinion, is her anger warranted? Why or why not?

_____

_____

2. What advice would you give to this teacher if she shared the afore-mentioned information with you?

_____

_____

CASE STUDY 10: A WELCOMING SCHOOL CLIMATE

After reading *Through Ebony Eyes,* a new teacher wrote the following question:

> "What are some strategies that educators can use to help parents feel included in the school setting and welcome on campus?"

1. How would you answer this teacher's question?

_____

_____

REVISITING CASE STUDIES 9 AND 10

For Case Study 9, the first thing I would do would be to empathize with the angry and frustrated teacher. I would say the following:

> I understand your frustration and anger. In fact, I remember times when I felt the same way when I was a high school teacher. Sometimes, only three or four parents would show up for "Back to School Night." I'd become frustrated. After teaching all day, then after going home to spend time with my family and eating dinner, I'd have to turn around and drive 30 miles back to my school site in order to attend "Back to School Night," and only a handful of parents would show up. However, I eventually realized that I could stay angry, or I could change my attitude. Changing my attitude was what I decided to do. I eventually realized that it was healthier for me to let go of my anger about what I perceived to be a lack of parent involvement and focus, instead, on the things that I could control:

- how I viewed students,
- whether or not I treated students fairly and humanely,
- the manner in which I explained and presented the subject matter that I was being paid to teach,
- whether or not I made my lesson plans interesting and relevant,
- whether or not I created a classroom climate that allowed students to learn in a safe and orderly environment,

- the amount of time that I was willing to invest in helping struggling students,
- the way that I treated parents, and
- giving extra credit to the students whose parents did come to events, as a way of rewarding the students, and also as an incentive to encourage other students to strongly encourage their parents to come.

The second to the last point, "the way that I treated parents," relates to how I would address Case Study 10. If a teacher asked me "What are some strategies that educators can use to help parents feel included in the school setting and welcome on campus?" I would tell that teacher that she had asked a great question and that it's wonderful that she is concerned about making parents feel welcome on campus. I would also tell this teacher that because many African American parents have had negative K–12 school experiences themselves, and also with their children's teachers and school administrators, how this teacher chooses to view and treat African American parents can improve or worsen relations between the teacher and parents. Because many African American parents view the school as hostile territory, in order to diffuse tension, I would also advise the teacher to do the following:

- Send cards or notes home to parents to inform them of their child's good behavior and positive accomplishments periodically, so that the parent isn't only hearing from the teacher when something negative happens.
- Telephone parents before situations escalate in order to make it clear that the teacher is concerned about the child's academic and personal welfare.
- During telephone calls and face-to-face meetings, begin by informing the parent of the areas where the student is doing well behaviorally and academically.
- Always be courteous to parents.
- Do not use academic jargon or multisyllabic words that are designed to make the parent feel inferior.
- Don't make assumptions about how much or how little the parent cares about the child's academic welfare merely because the parent doesn't attend school functions or because the child misbehaves in class or doesn't turn in his or her work.
- If you know that a parent is coming to campus to meet with you, inform the office staff and school security ahead of time in order to increase the likelihood that they will treat the parent respectfully when she or he arrives.
- If possible, meet the parent in the school office, greet the parent by name, introduce yourself, shake her or his hand, and escort the parent to your classroom.

Please respond to each question as honestly as possible.

1. At this point, how confident are you about your ability to use the curriculum to empower African American students?

   _____

   _____

2. How confident are you about your ability to help other teachers use the curriculum to empower African American students, and why?

   _____

   _____

★   ★   ★   ★   ★

The two case studies that you are about to read will, hopefully, boost your confidence about your ability to give advice to colleagues who come to you for help regarding how they can use the curriculum to empower African American students. The case studies will also allow you to *operationalize*, or actually use, what you've learned about the curriculum.

CASE STUDY 11: LOW EXPECTATIONS

After reading *Through Ebony Eyes,* a new teacher wrote the following:

> This has been my first year teaching. I have made countless mistakes along the way. One particularly trying experience has been with [one of my classes]. After an uneven, often trying first semester, I made the mistake of lowering my expectations. I was overwhelmed by the lack of skills, motivation, and perceived aptitude. How can I fix this? How do I stop this from happening again? What if you put the bar too high? Can you ever put the bar too high?

   1. If this teacher came to you for advice, what would you tell him or her?

   _____

   _____

CASE STUDY 12: TOO MUCH TO DO

Another teacher shared the following information with me after reading *Through Ebony Eyes:*

> [My problem is how to teach] as much as possible of the state standards, but still meet my school district's curriculum, and prepare freshmen for the new state competency test they have to pass before graduating.
>
> My district expects us to teach a lot of literature, plus a number of writing styles, plus prepare them for all the upcoming tests. It's too much. Something has to give and I'm inclined to cut out some of the core literature. I'm not sure what is the best route to take.

1. What advice would you give to this teacher?

_____

_____

REVISITING CASE STUDIES 11 AND 12

Case Studies 11 and 12 focus on common problems that many teachers experience. In Case Study 11, a first-year teacher lamented the fact that she lowered her expectations, and she asked questions about whether or not it's possible to have expectations that are too high. If this teacher came to me for advice, I would begin by commending her for her honesty in admitting that she had made a mistake by lowering her standards. I would also inform her that her experience isn't unusual. Many new teachers, and even those who have taught for longer periods, have felt overwhelmed when they learned that their students didn't have the skills that they'd expected and that their students appeared to be unmotivated. As I've mentioned previously, many African American K–12 students have historically been subjected to inequality of educational opportunity. The same is true of other students of color, such as Latinos, and also low-income students. Therefore, many students are subjected to grade inflation and low expectations—and are passed through the school system with below-grade-level skills.

Like this first-year teacher, many educators find it easier to merely lower their standards since the students are often performing way below grade level. However, what I would recommend to this teacher is that she continue to have high standards for all students. In order to determine whether or not she has set the bar too high, I'd suggest that she compare her expectations to the state standards for her grade level and make sure that her standards aren't lower or higher than these standards. Next, I would suggest that she use the "Theory of Small Wins," which merely suggests that she should help students reach the goals that she has set for them through small steps and small accomplishments. For example, if her ultimate goal is to help her students meet the algebra standards for the grade level that she teaches, she could break the goal down into small steps using the order of operations as her guide. This would require her to ensure that all students know how to add, subtract, divide, multiply, work with exponents, work with signed numbers, and work with problems enclosed in parentheses. Doing an assessment at the beginning of the year in the form of a quiz that includes addition, sub-traction, multiplication, division, signed numbers, parentheses, and exponents is an easy way of ascertaining whether or not students have the prerequisite skills they need in order to do algebra problems. After determining the types of math skills that students lack, the teacher can design her lesson plans, quizzes, and other activities around these skills and, at the same time, be headed toward her ultimate goal of helping students master algebra.

Case Study 12 also reveals a common problem: Many teachers feel overwhelmed by the demands that are placed on them. Since the pas-sage of the No Child Left Behind Act, and the related emphasis on stan-dardized tests, I have heard numerous teachers complain that they feel overwhelmed and aren't able to be as creative as they'd like because everything is about standards and testing. The advice that I give to these teachers is similar to what I would say to the teacher in Case Study 12: "Teach thematically." The late Margaret Goss, an African American veteran teacher, friend of mine, and mentor teacher, taught me this during my first year as a high school teacher. Teaching themat-ically requires teachers to identify several big ideas, themes, or con-cepts that they want to design their lessons around. Teachers can pick one theme per quarter or two themes per quarter, depending on their preference. But each theme should allow the teacher to create lesson plans that are tied to the state standards, and the lessons should be interesting, relevant, and empowering. For example, when I taught high school, I used themes such as "poverty," "discrimination," and "abuse" to teach reading, writing, speaking, and listening skills. I incorporated many types of writing, including writing personal letters, business letters, poetry, short stories, responses to literature, essays, and research papers into the thematic unit. All of the reading assign-ments, writing assignments, vocabulary exercises, quizzes, tests, and projects were tied directly or indirectly to the theme. I loved thematic teaching because it allowed me to use creativity in my lesson plans and, at the same time, make the lessons interesting and relevant to students' lives. In terms of whether or not the teacher should eliminate some of the core literature, I would suggest that the teacher consider using excerpts from some of the works instead of having students read the whole book, or using a *jigsaw* activity by having groups of students read various works, create a related audio-visual presentation for the whole class, and then present it in class. That would give all students exposure to all of the core literature without them having to read every single work individually.

EXERCISE 8F: REMEMBERING WHAT YOU'VE LEARNED ABOUT CLASSROOM MANAGEMENT

Please respond to each question as honestly as possible.

1. At this point, how confident are you about your ability to create a classroom climate in which your African American K–12 students can learn in a safe and orderly environment, and why?

   _____

   _____

2. How confident are you about your ability to help other teachers improve their classroom management skills, particularly in order to increase their efficacy with African American students, and why?

   _____

   _____

★　★　★　★　★

The next two case studies will give you opportunities to serve as an expert on classroom management.

CASE STUDY 13: A WELCOMING CLASSROOM ENVIRONMENT

A white female teacher in the 20- to 29-year-old age range wrote the following two questions on her "Searching for Solutions" questionnaire:

> "What do I do if a student has come in absolutely certain that I am like 'every other teacher' regardless of my actions? How can I produce a classroom where they feel more welcome if they are the only African American?"

1. What advice would you give her?

_____

_____

CASE STUDY 14: A PROBLEMATIC STUDENT

An Asian American student–teacher wrote the following after reading *Through Ebony Eyes:*

> The norm may be that African Americans speak loudly, and are sent mixed messages at school because they may be told to speak softer. I see this problem in the school I teach at. We have one African American student, and he is always calling out answers and speaking when the teacher is speaking. He gets put on time-outs and his mother is called in for conferences because of this issue. My question is "How can a teacher deal with such an issue without being too callous or lenient on a student?"

1. What advice would you give her?

_____

_____

REVISITING CASE STUDIES 13 AND 14

In Case Study 13, a teacher asked what she could do to convince students that she wasn't like "every other teacher." She also wanted to know how she could "produce a classroom where they feel more welcome if they are the only African American." If this teacher came to me for advice, I would tell her that because many African American students have negative school experiences, it is possible that when they finally get a good, caring teacher, they may assume that this teacher will view and treat them like their previous teachers have. However, if she is fair, consistent, and clear in articulating and enforcing her class rules, and makes the curriculum interesting and relevant, she will eventually earn the trust of most African American students. Over time, her reputation will precede her. In other words, other African American students will hear good things about her even before they are placed in her class, and she will find less resistance from most of these students. This teacher can increase the chances that all students, even the lone African American student, will feel welcome in her classroom if she sets a tone that indicates that this is her goal. That means that she will not permit students to make stereotypical comments, racial slurs, or refuse to sit next to or work with the lone African American student during group work. She will insist that this student be included in all class activities and be treated humanely and respectfully by his or her classmates.

Case Study 14 pertains to "loudness," a topic that often comes up when I conduct classroom management workshops for educators. In *Through Ebony Eyes* and *Up Where We Belong,* I spent a lot of time explaining that (1) many educators mistakenly assume that all African American students are loud; (2) often, educators knowingly or unwittingly single African American students out for being loud or for excessive talking while ignoring these very same behaviors when white students and other students engage in them; and (3) African American students often complain about this differential teacher treatment. So, if this student–teacher came to me for advice, I would first ask her several questions because her story raises a red flag for me. I find it hard to believe that, after repeatedly being punished for talking out of turn or speaking when the teacher is talking, the African American student would continue to behave this way. Therefore, I would ask the student–teacher the following questions:

- Is it really true that this student is "always calling out answers and speaking when the teacher is speaking," or does he do this occasionally?
- Is this student the only student who engages in this behavior?
- Has the teacher and student–teacher become accustomed to *looking for* trouble from this student to the point that they magnify or over-react to his behavior when they may unknowingly ignore similar behavior by other students?
- Is it possible that the African American student has inferred that the only way that he will get attention from his teacher is to behave in a negative manner? For example, when he does attempt to follow the rules and raise his hand before speaking, does the teacher ever call on him to do so?
- Does this student ever hear praise when he follows the rules?

The main reason I would first ask these questions is because I know that many African American boys have historically been demonized in American society and in schools. As I have stated in my previous books, and other researchers such as Dr. Jawanza Kunjufu,[1] Dr. Ann Arnett Ferguson,[2] Dr. Janice Hale,[3] Dr. Pedro Noguera,[4] and others have found, many African American high-achieving boys have extremely negative school experiences that dissuade them from staying on a positive academic course.[5] Even African American male high school students say that this demonization stems from teachers' fear of and ignorance about African American male students. As one African American male who participated in the *Up Where We Belong* study explained:

Teachers follow the stereotypes, like the students. . . . So, what's the first thing you do when you're intimidated? Try to get rid of the problem. That is fear. So, they try to get rid of the student. They discriminate against the student because he is Black and they're intimidated by him. The way they try to get rid of the problem is that as soon as that student messes up—the first thing—bam! He's outta there. A student could talk outta turn or something and get in trouble.[6]

After sharing this information with the teacher, I would address her question of "How can a teacher deal with such an issue without being too callous or lenient on a student?" I would ask her to use the same standard that she would use if she were dealing with an upper-class white student who was talking out of turn and, also, to treat the student in the same manner that she would want her own child's teacher to treat her son or daughter. In other words, I would remind her of the importance of treating students fairly and being consistent in enforcing class rules.

EXERCISE 8G: REMEMBERING WHAT YOU'VE LEARNED ABOUT TESTING

Please respond to each question as honestly as possible.

1. At this point, how confident are you about your ability to do a good job of preparing African American K–12 students for standardized tests, and why?

   _____

2. How confident are you about your ability to help other teachers do a better job of preparing African American students for standardized tests, and why?

   _____

CASE STUDY 15: THE EXAM IS APPROACHING

Regarding testing, a teacher asked the following:

"My freshmen students are taking the High School Exit Exam next month. Do you have any ideas about how I can prepare them for the language arts section?"

1. What advice would you give to this teacher?

   _____

   _____

CASE STUDY 16: MOTIVATING STUDENTS

On her "Searching for Solutions" questionnaire, a white female teacher in the 30- to 39-year-old age range wrote:

"How can I get buy-in from students to do their best on everything, including testing? I need solutions."

1. What advice would you give to this teacher?

_____

_____

REVISITING CASE STUDIES 15 AND 16

In Case Study 15, a freshmen language arts teacher wanted to know how to prepare her students for the High School Exit Exam. The problem was that she only had one month left before the exam would be given. The first thing that I would tell her would be to find out as much information as she could about the exam. The State Education Department in most, if not all, states has Web sites that usually contain extensive information about all state-mandated tests. If sample questions are available, this teacher could use this information to develop practice tests. If practice tests are already available, this would be even more helpful to her, especially given the time constraint that she faced. I would also urge her to use the State Education Department's Web site to review the language arts standards and objectives for ninth grade. The lesson plans that the teacher develops to prepare students for the exit exam should also revolve around these standards. Of course, during this month of test preparation, she would also need to teach students important test-taking strategies, such as how to read long passages and answer related questions, and she should make sure that her students know how to identify the plot, setting, main characters, theme, and so on, of literary passages. Guiding the class through one or more practice tests and explicitly teaching them the best strategies to use for each section of the test would allow the teacher to model test-taking strategies.

In addition to suggesting that the teacher also review the main rules of grammar, I would encourage her to plan ahead in the future. In other words, I would suggest that during the next year, she not wait until one month before an important state-mandated test was scheduled to be given to start preparing her students. African American students need their teachers to spend an adequate amount of time on test preparation. This is a point that I would also emphasize to the teacher in Case Study 16.

Case Study 16 is based on a question from a teacher who asked "How can I get buy-in from students to do their best on everything, including testing? I need solutions." If this teacher came to me for advice, I would share with her the main points that I covered in Chapter 7 of this book. I would inform her that her own attitude about standardized tests can have a negative effect on students if she gives mixed messages or unwittingly gives "negative test vibes." I would also encourage her to set the right tone in her classroom about testing by ensuring that the classroom environment is one that allows students to work in a safe and orderly environment. In addition to encouraging her to spend enough time on test preparation throughout the school year by incorporating test-taking strategies into the curriculum on an ongoing basis, and giving practice tests regularly, I would suggest that she also help students deal with test anxiety.

MOVING FORWARD

Now that you have served in the role of an expert on many topics pertaining to African American K–12 students, I hope that you (1) learned some new information about the areas where you feel most knowledgeable and those that you need to work on, (2) learned how you might assist a colleague who comes to you for help, and (3) had a chance to review some of the main points that I covered in previous chapters. But I can't let you off the hook yet. I'm going to conclude this chapter with one more case study. Case Study 17 is designed to help you apply most of the information that you've learned from this book to a practical, real-life scenario.

CASE STUDY 17: GROUP ACTIVITY FOR PROFESSIONAL DEVELOPMENT AND COURSE WORK

The following question was included in a letter that an Asian American teacher-education student sent to me after she read *Through Ebony Eyes:*

> "What do you think is the one most important thing educators need to know when educating black students?"

1. Before you read the last paragraph of this chapter, in small groups, create a response to this prospective teacher's question.

2. Share your responses with the larger group.

3. Now, read my response that follows, and then, compare and contrast your group's response to my own.

HOW I WOULD RESPOND

I wish that I could hear or read your answer(s) to this question. I also wish that I could ask you if it was easy or difficult for you to answer this question. If it was difficult for you, this wouldn't surprise me, because guess what? Answering this question was difficult for me, and I'm supposed to be an expert on how educators can improve the school experiences of African American students!

It wasn't difficult for me because I couldn't think of *anything* to say. In fact, the opposite is true. I had so much to say that I didn't know where to begin. However, I couldn't say everything that I wanted to say because the woman in Case Study 17 asked me to only reveal "the one most important thing." Therefore, that limited my options. So, if this individual asked me for advice, and I could only tell her one thing, I would tell her what I've said in several of my other books and what I often say in the workshops that I conduct for educators: "Treat African American students in the way in which you would want your own children's teachers to treat your children." Teachers who do this will, undoubtedly, make mistakes along the way, but they will hold themselves to what is, in my opinion, the highest standard that a teacher can have for himself or herself.

Conclusion

A Work in Progress: Committing to Ongoing Personal and Professional Development

Throughout this book, you have read stories, research, and strategies, and you have completed numerous exercises that I designed to help you increase your efficacy with African American K–12 students. As I said in the Introduction, as educators, "alarm bells should be ringing in our heads" because despite all of the progress that has been made in various sectors of the United States, many African American K–12 students continue to have extremely negative school experiences, as reflected by dropout rates, graduation rates, standardized test scores, and the number of African American students who get trapped in the school-to-prison pipeline.

If you were able to read this entire book from cover to cover and complete all of the exercises, let me commend you for your courage and persistence. By now, you should be well on your way to working effectively with African American K–12 students and their parents. More than anything, you should be in a position to reverse the negative trend of African American underachievement that is so common in many schools. Specifically, I hope that you have

- faced and eradicated any mental baggage that you had about African American students and their parents,
- learned important lessons about how racism can harm African American students,
- learned how to better use the curriculum to empower African American students,
- improved your classroom management skills,

- understood the value of improving your relations with African American parents and learned specific ways to do this,
- understood the ways in which you can better prepare African American students for standardized tests, and
- identified the personal benefits of choosing to increase your efficacy with African American students.

Four of the main points that I would like you to remember from the studies that I conducted for this book are as follows:

- Many teachers don't know how to work effectively with African American students.
- Many teachers do not believe that African American students are as intelligent as nonblack students.
- Many teachers and school principals don't believe that African American K–12 students are capable of academic excellence.
- Many teachers have very low expectations of African American students.

These mindsets and issues are pernicious problems that affect countless African American students and increase their chances of receiving a substandard education that will prevent them from improving the quality of their lives. The information you have learned should help you to not perpetuate inequality of educational opportunity through your beliefs and actions. The information that you've learned also puts you in a position to be able to help teachers who may one day come to you for help, like the ones whom you read about in Chapter 8.

However, regardless of how much you have grown from the information that you have learned, you are not, nor will you ever be, a "perfect" educator of African American students. Humans—even well-informed educators—are imperfect. In other words, there's still a lot of work left for you to do. For this reason, I am going to ask you to make a commitment to engage in ongoing personal and professional development so that you will continue to increase your efficacy with African American students. I would like to challenge you to continue to do the following:

- Keep a journal about your thoughts and experiences with African American students and parents.
- Make a commitment to read the books and articles that I cited in previous chapters.
- Continue to look for the personal benefits of increasing your efficacy with African American students.
- Share what you've learned with other educators, especially new teachers.

A FINAL STORY

I want to conclude this book with a story that I heard in 2009. Shortly before I was scheduled to give a presentation at a prestigious Catholic high school in northern California, I heard a fascinating story that another guest speaker at this same school shared. The other guest speaker, a white grandmother, wanted educators to understand the lessons that she had learned about race relations and working with African American students. When I heard her speak, I knew instantly that her story would be the perfect way to end this book. Although she gave me permission to retell her story, she asked that I refrain from using her real name. So to protect her identity, I will refer to her as Ann.

A WHITE GRANDMOTHER'S MESSAGE TO EDUCATORS: "I TREATED THEM MORE LIKE THEY WERE *MY* CHILDREN."

Ann's personal-growth journey, which changed her outlook about African Americans and prompted her to improve the school and life experiences of youth, began 20 years ago. At the time, she was a housewife and the mother of a daughter who was a high school senior. She also had two young sons. During this period, three events had a profound effect on her: She heard a speech that urged listeners to "get out of their comfort zone;" she read a book about Mother Teresa; and an African American acquaintance who was the director of an "all-black gym" that offered sports' programs to children in the community invited her to visit the gym. After several invitations, Ann reluctantly accepted his offer, and one day, she and one of her sons showed up at the gym. "I was scared to death," Ann admitted.

But in spite of her fear, Ann and her son entered the gym. "I walked into the gym with my young, blond son," she said. An African American boy hurried over to them and made her son feel welcome. Ann was so grateful for the child's overture of friendship that from that moment on, she stated, "I decided that if that black kid, Bruce, ever needed anything, I would help him."

Although she didn't know it at the moment when she made that decision, she would be seeing a lot more of Bruce and the other African American children at that gym. It turned out that her son had made friends so quickly, and enjoyed the visit so much, that he wanted to join the gym's program. This meant that what Ann had only thought would be *one* visit ended up becoming a regular part of Ann and her son's life.

After that first visit, the gym became Ann's classroom—a place where she learned new information and began to interact with African Americans on a regular basis. "You can learn a lot just by sitting, watching, and listening. Just keep your mouth shut," she stated. One day, a little African American girl asked Ann what she was doing at the gym. When Ann told her that she was waiting for her son, the girl asked her which child was her son. As she shared this memory with the audience on the day I heard her speak, Ann chuckled at the innocence of children. Although her son was the only white child at the gym, and a blond one on top of that, the girl had asked her to point him out.

The more she listened, observed, and spoke with the youth and their parents, the more Ann began to realize how different these children's lives were from the privileged lives of her own children. The African American kids attended substandard schools. Her own children had attended private schools and were definitely being groomed for college. Eventually Ann realized that "these kids need to feel like they can get out of the community." But more than anything, she realized that she could play a role in improving their future. After all, her own daughter, the high school senior, had not only befriended a student from another country but also went out of her way to help him. In order to help him improve his English skills, her daughter offered to tutor him, and she also began to invite him to family functions and various events to assist him in acclimating to the United States.

Therefore, Ann decided to use the resources that she had. "I was a stay at home mom who had raised children. I had no credentials," she explained. Nevertheless, she believed that what she knew about child rearing could be used to help the African American children. According to Ann, "The test of individual responsibility is, are we willing to do something about [a problem]?"

Like her daughter, Ann started by inviting African American children from the gym to various events in order to give them opportunities to experience life outside of their community. She took them to see "The Nutcracker," ballets, and plays, and she took them on picnics. She also taught them how to swim, gave them birthday cards, and drove them to athletic events. "We just kind of spent time together," she explained. "I had a mother's plan. I didn't have a psychologist's plan. . . . I treated them more like they were my children. . . . This became my group of kids. Then, I started running a tutoring program at a community center." As the children got older, she even helped them find summer jobs—on a ranch in Idaho!

But Ann wasn't naïve. Even though the African American kids "almost became my own . . . I knew the statistics," she said. "My sons were going to go to college. They [the African Americans] might end up in prison, but they had hopes and dreams." Then, someone told her that if she could help the African American youth that she had been mentoring attend better schools, this would make a powerful impact on their lives. So she and her husband started sending African American boys to private Catholic middle schools.

Then, when it was time for her own son to enter the private high school that his sister had attended, Ann and her husband decided that they would also pay for his African American best friend to attend the school. This eventually became a trend, and year after year, Ann and her husband provided scholarships for numerous African American students to attend the prestigious school. But she did more than invest money in their education; she also continued to invest her time by visiting them regularly and encouraging them to do their best. Although it cost Ann and her husband about $3,000 per year to send each boy to Catholic school, starting when he was in middle school, she felt that it was worth the sacrifice. "They got used to being around other people, and they got used to getting out of their comfort zone, and turning in homework on time," she said.

Although many of the boys turned out well, not all did. Nevertheless, Ann still felt that her time, money, and effort were worthwhile. "You're in the job of imputing. You're not in the job of seeing results," she explained. One of the most important lessons that she learned was that, sometimes, African American students have negative school experiences because they truly do not know how to be successful at school and have been underprepared for academic success. A good example pertains to one of the African American boys whom she sponsored to attend the Catholic high school.

This boy didn't obey the class rules, had weak academic skills, and was viewed as a discipline problem. "He came from an unstable home," Ann explained. "He went to live with somebody else who got him to school on time. He walked about a mile to school. He never had a lunch, never had a breakfast. But there was something in that kid. He was resilient."

Nevertheless, after awhile, a school official warned Ann that she didn't know if this student would be able to remain at the school. But instead of giving up on him, Ann got him a tutor and spoke with him about the rules. Then, she realized that he didn't really know the rules. After a school official explained them to him, he ended up winning awards. When the boy was kicked out of the home in which he was living, a white teacher at the school and her African American husband agreed to let him move into their home. In the end, the student not only ended up graduating from the prestigious high school, but he also graduated from college and became a famous athlete. Today, he is a well-known basketball coach who remains grateful to Ann and the teacher who believed in him enough to put their words into actions.

I will conclude with several quotes that Ann wanted the educators who were in the audience that day to remember:

"Keep feeding students what they need, and just keep loving them."

"Young people want your heart. . . . They want to know 'Am I important to you?'"

"You do what's right. It doesn't matter if you feel
comfortable or not. You do what's right."

"It's been a wonderful adventure because I got out
of my comfort zone."

"You never know what's going to happen."

So let me conclude this book by wishing you the best as you continue on your journey to becoming an outstanding educator of African American K–12 students. If you continue on this quest, years from now, one or more of your African American former students might write about you one day, send you an e-mail, or search for you to say, "Thank you for being the educator who changed my life." Remember that you have the power to help or harm African American students. I hope that you will use your power for good.

Appendix A

The "What's In It for Me?" Questionnaire

INFORMATION ABOUT THE RESPONDENTS (N = 108)

1. Which of the following best describes your work with African American students?

a. I am a teacher.	12%
b. I am a school counselor.	2%
c. I am a principal or vice principal.	3%
d. I am a district level employee.	55%
e. Other	27%

2. If you are an educator, how long have you been an educator?

a. less than five years	4%
b. 5–10 years	13%
c. 11–20 years	19%
d. more than 20 years	28%

N = 69

3. What is your age group?

a. 30 years old or less	8%
b. 31–40 years old	28%
c. 41–50 years old	32%
d. 51 or older	29%

4. What is your race?

a. Native American	1%
b. Black, African American, African, black West Indian, etc.	32%
c. Latino, Chicano, Hispanic	10%
d. White, Anglo, Caucasian	52%
e. Asian American	5%

Appendix B

The "What's In It for Me?" Questionnaire Results

List three ways in which you would personally benefit from working more effectively with black students.

Response	%
I would understand students and parents better.	37
It would benefit society and/or the community.	37
I would feel better about myself.	31
I would become a better teacher.	24
It would improve students' futures.	20
I will have better relations with these students.	20
It would help the school in general.	14
It's a matter of equity, fairness, and morality.	13
It would empower students.	12
It would allow me to tap students' potential.	10
It will eliminate stereotypes.	9
All students would benefit.	8
It would improve students' test scores.	6
It would decrease discipline problems.	6
It would improve students' skills.	5

N = 108

Appendix C

What Educators Said They Believed About African American Students

Statement	True	False
1. I honestly believe that my African American students are capable of doing outstanding academic work.	67	2
2. I honestly believe that most of my African American students have caring parents or guardians.	66	3
3. I am just as confident about my ability to help my African American students do well in my class as I am about my ability to help my other students.	61	7
4. To be honest, I would prefer not to deal with African American students.	0	70
5. I truly believe that most of my African American students are just as smart as most of my other students.	68	1

N = 71 educators attending a workshop at an elementary school in southern California in 2007. Note: Totals that are less than 71 are caused by the number of participants who did not respond to a statement.

Appendix D

*Demographic Information About the Texas and
California Workshop Participants Who Completed
The Mindset Questionnaire (by %)*

	Texas	California
Administrators	55	0
Teachers	45	0
Preservice teachers	0	100
Males	17	28
Females	79	68
Whites	58	37
Nonwhites (including African Americans)	39	52
(African Americans)	32	6

Total N = 237. Percentage totals that are less than 100 can be explained by
the number of participants who did not respond to various questionnaire
items.

Appendix E

The Mindset Questionnaire Results (N = 237)

1. Most teachers know how to work effectively with African American K–12 students (by %).

	True	False
Preservice teachers	9	90
Teachers	6	94
Administrators	14	86
Whites	12	88
Nonwhites (including African Americans)	8	92
African Americans	2	98
Males	22	78
Females	7	93

2. In my opinion, most teachers believe that most African American K–12 students are capable of doing outstanding academic work (by %).

	True	False
Preservice teachers	29	70
Teachers	48	52
Administrators	41	57
Whites	46	53
Nonwhites (including African Americans)	30	68
African Americans	27	73
Males	56	42
Females	33	66

3. In my opinion, most school principals believe that most African American K–12 students are capable of doing outstanding academic work.

	True	False
Preservice teachers	32	65
Teachers	48	52
Administrators	52	48
Whites	49	49
Nonwhites (including African Americans)	37	62
African Americans	33	67
Males	62	38
Females	37	62

4. In my opinion, most teachers treat and view most African American K–12 students in the same ways that they treat and view most nonblack students.

	True	False
Preservice teachers	18	82
Teachers	23	77
Administrators	28	72
Whites	30	70
Nonwhites (including African Americans)	16	84
African Americans	2	98
Males	34	66
Females	21	79

5. In my opinion, most teachers believe that the parents or guardians of most African American K–12 students are very concerned about their education.

	True	False
Preservice teachers	21	78
Teachers	22	78
Administrators	15	84
Whites	17	82
Nonwhites (including African Americans)	22	77
African Americans	14	87
Males	34	64
Females	16	84

6. In my opinion, most teachers believe that most African American K–12 students are just as intelligent as most nonblack students.

	True	False
Preservice teachers	42	57
Teachers	48	50
Administrators	46	53
Whites	52	47
Nonwhites (including African Americans)	38	61
African Americans	23	75
Males	62	37
Females	40	60

7. What are the main reasons why many African American students do not do as well in school as they could?

	The Most Frequently Cited Factors (by %)			
	Low Teacher Expectations	Curriculum/ Teaching Methods	Racism	Parents
Total	56	46	27	27
Preservice Teachers	66	61	48	11
Practicing Teachers	45	34	14	39
Administrators	53	39	11	38
Whites	50	47	28	21
Nonwhites (including African Americans)	62	46	25	34
African Americans	54	35	17	50
Males	46	46	14	16
Females	59	48	31	32

8. What are the main reasons why many African American students do not do as well in school as they could?

Less Frequently Cited Factors (by %)

	Unfair Teachers	Peers	Home Life	Poor Relations With Teachers	Poverty
Total	22	19	19	15	13
Preservice Teachers	35	17	13	10	16
Practicing Teachers	14	27	25	11	9
Administrators	13	14	23	24	11
Whites	17	19	19	15	11
Nonwhites	27	19	20	14	14
African Americans	27	21	19	15	8
Males	20	24	20	12	20
Females	22	18	20	16	11

Appendix F

Demographic Information About the Workshop Participants Who Completed the "Searching for Solutions Questionnaire" (by %)

	Public Elementary	Private High School
Teachers	88	50
Administrators	6	22
Non-educators	6	22
Males	15	25
Females	79	64
Whites	42	50
Nonwhites	49	28

Total N = 69. Percentage totals that are less than 100 can be explained by the number of participants who did not respond to various questionnaire items.

Note: *Non-educators* refer to workshop participants who were not teachers or administrators but were affiliated with the school or school district in some other way (staff, school board member, etc.).

Appendix G

The "Searching for Solutions" Questionnaire Results (N = 69)

1. In your opinion, is it possible for educators to change negative mindsets and stereotypes that they have about African American students?

   Yes = 91% No = 1%

2. If it is possible, how can this be done?

   - Education/awareness/inservices for teachers   57%
   - Face biases/identify stereotypes/introspection   41%
   - Personal choice/commit to change   23%
   - Use the community, students, and parents as resources   16%
   - Improve teacher behavior and practices   15%

3. What, if any, are the main problems that you've experienced with African American students?

   - Bad attitude/anger/defensiveness   38%
   - None   26%
   - Low self-expectations/low self-esteem   25%
   - Other problems   25%
   - Apathy/disillusionment   10%
   - Poor academic work   9%
   - Lack of trust   7%

4. What questions or concerns do you still have about working with African American students? (Some of the answers to this question are presented in Chapter 8).

Appendix H

Demographic Information About the Workshop Participants Who Completed the "Thoughts About Racism and Racial Problems" Questionnaire (by %)

Teachers	70
Administrators	15
Non-educators	12
Males	13
Females	83
Whites	69
Nonwhites	26

Total N = 203

Note: *Non-educators* refers to workshop participants who were not teachers or administrators but were affiliated with the school or school district in some other way (staff, school board member, etc.).

Appendix I

The "Thoughts About Racism and Racial Problems"
Questionnaire (N = 203)

1. If you could ask three to five questions about race relations, racism, multi-culturalism, and cultural issues, what would you ask? (See Chapter 8 for some of the responses.)

2. In your opinion, are race relations in the United States
   a. better than they were when you were growing up?   37%
   b. about the same as they were when you were growing up?   47%
   c. worse than they were when you were growing up?   16%

3. How often do you think about racism and racial problems?
   a. often   56%
   b. sometimes   35%
   c. rarely   9%

4. In your opinion, what are the main causes of racial problems in the United States?
   - Old ideas/beliefs/stereotypes/biases   35%
   - Inequality/poverty/segregation/isolation   35%
   - Ignorance   27%
   - Education, or lack thereof   23%
   - Lack of interracial/cross-racial experiences and   18%
     interactions
   - Fear   18%
   - Misunderstandings   17%
   - Institutional racism   17%
   - Media/racial profiling   16%

- History   15%
- Adults/parents   14%
- Sense of entitlement/superiority/white supremacy   13%

5. Do you believe that racism will be eradicated during your lifetime?
   a. Yes   2%
   b. Unsure   14%
   c. No   83%

6. In your opinion, what will it take for racism and racial problems to be eradicated in the United States?
   - Better education   45%
   - More opportunities/eliminate economic barriers   29%
   - More dialogue/greater awareness   24%
   - Cross cultural/cross-racial interactions   21%
   - Better leadership   17%
   - Take personal responsibility   16%
   - Improve school system   12%
   - Avoid stereotyping/sensationalism   9%

Percentage totals that are less than 100 can be explained by the number of participants who did not respond to various questionnaire items. For some questions, respondents gave multiple answers.

Appendix J

The "Test" Questionnaire (N = 63)

1. List five strategies that teachers can use to prepare students for standardized tests.

The Most Frequently Cited Strategies (by %)

Model test-taking strategies	60
Give practice tests	48
Tie the curriculum to the information on which students will be tested	37
Teach students how to read test questions	33
Teach students how to select the best choice	22
Offer tutoring	18
Build students' confidence	18
Spend enough time on skill development	18

Less Frequently Cited Strategies (by %)

Teach students how to identify key words	15
Familiarize yourself with the test format	14
Reteach information	11
Focus on areas of weakness	11
Teach lessons in the test format	11
Teach concepts	11
Review information	10
Explain why the test is important	8

Use visuals	8
Use hands-on activities	8
Cover test objectives	6
Assess students at the beginning of the year	6
Devote enough time to test preparation	6
Use mnemonic devices	5
Give examples and sample questions	5
Teach students how to pace themselves	5
Help students deal with test anxiety	3
Encourage students to get enough sleep	3
Encourage students to eat breakfast	3

2. Which one of the following statements best reflects your views?

a. I am satisfied with the number of tests that K–12 students are required to take.	25
b. I believe that K–12 students are required to take too many tests.	58
c. I believe that K–12 students should be required to take fewer tests.	17

Demographic Information About the Respondents

Job Description

Teacher	58
School administrator	32
Other district or school employee	7
Other	2

Gender

Male	15
Female	85

Race

Black/African American	30
Latino/Chicano	3
Asian American	0
White	48

Note: Percentage totals that are less than 100 can be explained by the number of participants who did not respond to various questionnaire items.

Notes

Introduction

1. National Center for Education Statistics. *Fast facts*. Retrieved August 12, 2008, from http://nces.ed.gov/FastFacts/display.asp?id=16

2. Swanson, C. B. (2008). *Cities in crisis: A special analytic report on high school graduation*. Editorial Projects in Education Research Center. Retrieved August 12, 2008, from http://nces.ed.gov/FastFacts/display.asp?id=16

3. Ibid.

4. National Summary. *Ready for what? Preparing students for college, careers, and life after high school*. The Graduation Project 2007. Educational Projects in Education Research Center. Retrieved August 12, 2008, from http://www.edweek.org/media/ew/dc/2007/40national_SGB07.pdf

5. Ibid.

6. U.S. Census Bureau. *United States Educational Attainment. 2006 American Community Survey*. Retrieved August 12, 2008, from http://factfinder.census.gov/servlet/STTable?_bm=y&-geo_id=01000US&-qr_name=ACS_2006_EST_G00_S1501&-ds_name=ACS_2006_EST_G00_&-_lang=en&-redoLog=false&-CONTEXT=st

7. U.S. Census Bureau. *Income, poverty, and health insurance coverage in the United States: 2006*. Retrieved August 12, 2008, from http://www.census.gov/prod/2007pubs/p60–233.pdf

8. U.S. Department of Justice, Office of Justice Programs, Office of Juvenile Justice and Delinquency Prevention. Law enforcement & juvenile crime. *Statistical Briefing Book*. Retrieved August 12, 2008, from http://ojjdp.ncjrs.gov/ojstatbb/crime/faqs.asp

9. U. S. Department of Justice, Bureau of Justice Statistics. *Criminal offenders statistics*. Retrieved August 12, 2008, from http://www.ojp.usdoj.gov/bjs/crimoff.htm#lifetime, p. 1.

10. Ibid.

11. Ibid.

12. The Children's Defense Fund. (2008). *Cradle to prison pipeline fact sheet*. Retrieved August 12, 2008, from http://www.childrensdefense.org/site/DocServer/CPP_fact_sheet_4.15.08.pdf?docID=6201, p. 1

13. NAACP Legal Defense and Educational Fund, Inc. *Dismantling the school to prison pipeline*. Retrieved August 12, 2008, from http://www.naacpldf.org/content/pdf/pipeline/Dismantling_the_School_to_Prison_Pipeline.pdf, p. 2.

14. Ibid.

Chapter 1

1. Ruddell, R. (1998). *Teaching children to read and write: Becoming an influential teacher.* Columbus, OH: Allyn and Bacon.

2. Ibid.

3. Kozol, J. (2005). *The shame of the nation: The restoration of apartheid schooling in America.* New York: Crown Publishers.

4. Ellis, T. I. (1984). Motivating teachers for excellence. ERIC Clearinghouse on Educational Management: *ERIC Digest, Number Six.* Retrieved October 5, 2008, from http://www.ericdigests.org/pre-921/motivating.htm, p. 1.

5. Raffa Cuomo, M. (Ed.). (2002). *Who mentored you? The person who changed my life: Prominent people recall their mentors.* New York: Book-of-the-Month Club.

Chapter 2

1. McHugh, B. (October 6, 2006). "Is your personal baggage stuffing up your marriage?" *Mental Health Families.* Retrieved August 9, 2008, from http://mental-health.families.com/blog/is-your-personal-baggage-stuffing-up-your-marriage, p. 1.

2. Gay, G. (2000). *Culturally responsive teaching: Theory, research, and practice.* New York: Teachers College Press; Kunjufu, J. (2002). *Black students/middle class teachers.* Chicago: African American Images; Ladson-Billings, G. (2002). I ain't writin' nuttin': Permissions to fail and demands to succeed in urban classrooms. In L. Delpit & J. Kilgour Dowdy (Eds). *The skin that we speak: Thoughts on language and culture in the classroom* (pp. 109–120). New York: The New Press; Landsman, J. (2004). Confronting the racism of low expectations: Racism in educators' attitudes—and in how students are placed in advanced classes—still robs minority students of chances for success. *Educational Leadership*, November, 28–32.

3. Delpit, L. (1995). *Other people's children: Cultural conflict in the classroom.* New York: The New Press; Gay, G. (2000). *Culturally responsive teaching: Theory, research, and practice.* New York: Teachers College Press; Landsman, J. (2004). Confronting the racism of low expectations: Racism in educators' attitudes—and in how students are placed in advanced classes—still robs minority students of chances for success. *Educational Leadership*, 62(3), 28–32.

4. Comer, J. P. (2004). *Leave no child behind: Preparing today's youth for tomorrow's world.* New Haven, CT: Yale University Press; Ladson-Billings, G. (1994). *The dreamkeepers: Successful teachers of African American children.* San Francisco: Jossey Bass; Yau, R. (2002). High-achieving elementary schools with large percentages of low-income African American students: A review and critique of the current research. In S. J. Denbo & L. Moore Beaulieu (Eds.). *Improving schools for African American students: A reader for educational leaders*, 193–217. Springfield, IL: Charles C. Thomas Publisher.

5. Delpit, L. (1995). *Other people's children: Cultural conflict in the classroom*. New York: The New Press; Gay, G. (2000). *Culturally responsive teaching: Theory, research, and practice*. New York: Teachers College Press; Ladson-Billings, G. (1994). *The dreamkeepers: Successful teachers of African American children*. San Francisco: Jossey Bass.

6. Aronson, J. (2004). The threat of stereotype: To close the achievement gap, we must address negative stereotypes that suppress student achievement. *Educational Leadership, 62*(3), 14–19; Comer, J. P. (2004). *Leave no child behind: Preparing today's youth for tomorrow's world*. New Haven, CT: Yale University Press; Drew, D. E. (1996). *Aptitude revisited: Rethinking math and science education for America's next century*. Baltimore: The Johns Hopkins University Press.

7. Thompson, G. L. (2004). *Through ebony eyes: What teachers need to know but are afraid to ask about African American students*. San Francisco: Jossey Bass.

8. Bonilla-Silva, E. (2003). *Racism without racists: Color-blind racism and the persistence of racial inequality in the United States*. Lanham, MD: Rowman & Littlefield Publishers; Hale, J. E. (2001). *Learning while black: Creating educational excellence for African American children*. Baltimore: The Johns Hopkins University Press; Kozol, J. (2005). *The shame of a nation: The restoration of apartheid schooling in America*. New York: Crown Publishers; Kunjufu, J. (2005). *Keeping black boys out of special education*. Chicago: African American Images.

9. Phillips Academy Andover. About Andover overview and history. Retrieved August 19, 2008, from http://www.andover.edu/About/PAToday/Pages/default.aspx

10. Phillips Academy Andover. About Andover statement of purpose. Retrieved August 19, 2008, from http://www.andover.edu/About/PAToday/Pages/StatementofPurpose.aspx

11. Sue, D. W. (2003). *Overcoming our racism: The journey to liberation*. San Francisco: Jossey Bass.

12. Gardner, H. (2006). *Changing minds: The art and science of changing our own and other people's minds*. Boston: Harvard Business School Press.

13. Dombeck, M., & Wells-Moran, J. Applying learning principles to thought: Cognitive restructuring. *MentalHelp.net*. Retrieved October 15, 2008, from http://www.mentalhelp.net/poc/view_doc.php?type=doc&id=9746&cn=353, p. 1.

14. Beck, J. (2007). *The Beck diet solution: Train your brain to think like a thin person*. Birmingham, AL: Oxmoor House.

15. Dombeck, M., & Wells-Moran, J. Cognitive restructuring. *MentalHelp.net*. Retrieved October 15, 2008, from http://www.mentalhelp.net/poc/view_doc.php?type=doc&id=9749&cn=353

16. Dombeck, M., & Wells-Moran, J. Applying learning principles to thought: Cognitive restructuring. *MentalHelp.net*. Retrieved October 15, 2008, from http://www.mentalhelp.net/poc/view_doc.php?type=doc&id=9746&cn=353

17. Ibid., 1.

18. Dombeck, M., & Wells-Moran, J. Common types of thought and belief mistakes. *MentalHelp.net.* Retrieved October 15, 2008, from http://www.mentalhelp.net/poc/view_doc.php?type=doc&id=9747&cn=353

19. Dombeck, M., & Wells-Moran, J. Applying learning principles to thought: Cognitive restructuring. *MentalHelp.net.* Retrieved October 15, 2008, from http://www.mentalhelp.net/poc/view_doc.php?type=doc&id=9746&cn=353, p. 1.

Chapter 3

1. CNN.com. (2006, December 12). Poll: Most Americans see lingering racism—in others. Retrieved January 25, 2009, from http://www.cnn.com/2006/US/12/12/racism.poll/index.html, p. 1.

2. Sue, D. W. (2003). *Overcoming our racism: The journey to liberation.* San Francisco: Jossey Bass.

3. Ibid.

4. Trepagnier, B. (2006). *Silent racism: How well-meaning white people perpetuate the racial divide.* Boulder, CO: Paradigm Publishers.

5. Sue, D. W. (2003). *Overcoming our racism: The journey to liberation.* San Francisco: Jossey Bass.

6. Johnson Rice, L. (2009, February). Black history/black love: A message from the chairman and CEO. *Ebony.* p. 14.

7. Nagourney, A. (2008, July 16). Poll Finds Obama Isn't Closing Divide on Race. *NY Times.* Retrieved January 25, 2009, from http://www.nytimes.com/2008/07/16/us/politics/16poll.html?_r=2&hp=&oref=slogin&pagewanted

8. Ibid.

9. hooks, b. (2003). *Rock my soul: Black people and self-esteem.* New York: Atria Books.

10. Boyd-Franklin, N. (2003). *Black families in therapy: Understanding the African American experience* (2nd ed.). New York: The Guilford Press.

11. Levin, A. (December 15, 2006). Battling depression among blacks means confronting racism's legacy. *Psychiatric News.* 41(24), 4. Retrieved November 15, 2006, from http://pn.psychiatryonline.org/cgi/content/full/41/24/4-a

12. Boyd-Franklin, N. (2003). *Black families in therapy: Understanding the African American experience* (2nd ed.). New York: The Guilford Press; Suddreth, L. D. (1993). How racism affects everyone: Alvin Poussaint Delivers Keynote Address. Retrieved November 15, 2006, from http://www.loc.gov/loc/lcib/93/ 9304/racism.html

13. Thompson, G. L. (2003). *What African American parents want educators to know.* Westport, CT: Greenwood.

14. Cohen, C. J., Celestine-Michener, J., Holmes, C., Merseth, J. L., & Ralph, L. (February, 2007). Black youth project. A research project exploring the attitudes, actions and decision-making of African American youth by highlighting their lives, ideas, and voices. Retrieved June 5, 2007, from www.blackyouthproject.com, 19.

Chapter 4

1. Time Life Books Editors. (1994). *African Americans: Voices of Triumph:* ~~L~~ heritage of African leadership, science and invention, business and industry, r~~e~~.~~c~~ education, politics. Alexandria, VA: Time-Life Books.

2. Horton, J. O., & Horton, L. E. (2001). *Hard road to freedom: The story of African America*. New Brunswick, N J: Rutgers University Press.

3. Anderson, C. (1994). *Black labor, white wealth: The search for power and economic justice*. Bethesda, MD: PowerNomics Corporation of America.

4. Anderson, J. D. (1988). *The education of blacks in the South: 1860–1935*. Chapel Hill: The University of North Carolina Press; Du Bois, W. E. B. (1935). *Black reconstruction in America: 1860–1880*. New York: Atheneum; Franklin, J. H. (2005). *Mirror to America: The autobiography of John Hope Franklin*. New York: Farrar, Straus, and Giroux; Johnson, C. (1938). *The negro college graduate*. New York: Negro Universities Press.

5. Du Bois, W. E. B. (1935). *Black reconstruction in America: 1860–1880*. New York: Atheneum, p. 637.

6. Du Bois, W. E. B. (1910). *The college-bred negro*. Atlanta: The Atlanta University Press.

7. Anderson, J. D. (1988). *The education of blacks in the south: 1860–1935*. Chapel Hill: The University of North Carolina Press.

8. Thompson, G. L. (November, 2009). *A brighter day: How parents can help African American youth*. Chicago: African American Images.

9. Thompson, G. L. (2003). *What African American parents want educators to know*. Westport, CT: Greenwood.

10. Thompson, G. L. (2007). *Up where we belong: Helping African American and Latino students rise in school and in life*. San Francisco: Jossey Bass.

11. Thompson, G. L. (2003). *What African American parents want educators to know*. Westport, CT: Greenwood.

12. Clark, R. (1983). *Family life and school achievement: Why poor black children succeed or fail*. Chicago: University of Chicago Press.

13. Thompson, G. L. (2003). *What African American parents want educators to know*. Westport, CT: Greenwood; Thompson, G. L. (2007). *Up where we belong: Helping African American and Latino students rise in school and in life*. San Francisco: Jossey Bass.

14. National PTA. (2000). *A guide to developing parent and family· programs*. Bloomington, IN: National Educational Service.

15. Henderson, A. T., Johnson, V., Mapp, K., & Davies, D. (2007). *Beyond the bake sale: The essential guide to family/school partnerships*. New York: New Press.

Chapter 5

1. McEwan, E. (2002). *Teach them all to read: Catching the kids who fall through the cracks*. Thousand Oaks, CA: Corwin.

2. Lehr, C. A. (2004). Improving graduation results: Strategies for addressing today's needs. *Impact: Feature Issue on Achieving Secondary Education and Transition Results for Students with Disabilities, 16*(3). Retrieved February 11, 2009, from http://ici .umn.edu/products/impact/163/over4.html, p. 1.

3. Stull, J. (2001). Kindergarten teachers' use of computers in the classroom. *Techno Brief.* Retrieved February 11, 2009, from http://www.temple.edu/martec/ publications/technobriefs/tbrief6.html

4. National Center on Secondary Education and Transition. *Part 1: What do we know about dropout prevention?* Retrieved February 11, 2009, from http://www.ncset .org/publications/essentialtools/dropout/part1.3.asp

5. Thompson, G. L. (2002). *African American teens discuss their schooling experiences.* Westport, CT: Bergin & Garvey.

6. Almond, M. (2009, January 31). My journey to this moment in history: The inauguration of Barack Obama. *Claremont Courier*, pp. 20–21.

7. Delpit, L. (1995). *Other people's children: Cultural conflict in the classroom.* New York: The New Press; Gay, G. (2000). *Culturally responsive teaching: Theory, research, and practice.* New York: Teachers College Press; Ladson-Billings, G. (1994). *The dreamkeepers: Successful teachers of African American children.* San Francisco: Jossey Bass.

8. Hale, J. E. (2001). *Learning while black: Creating educational excellence for African American children.* Baltimore: The Johns Hopkins University Press.

9. Drew, D. E. (1996). *Aptitude revisited: Rethinking math and science education for America's next century.* Baltimore: Johns Hopkins University Press.

10. Benard, B. (2004). Resiliency: *What we have learned.* San Francisco: WestEd.

Chapter 6

1. U.S. Department of Education, Institute of Education Sciences. (n.d.). *Digest of education statistics: 2007. Table 68. Teachers' perceptions about serious problems in their schools, by control and level of school: 1993–94, 1999–2000, and 2003–04.* National Center of Education Statistics. Retrieved February 25, 2009, from http://nces.ed .gov/programs/digest/d07/tables/dt07_068.asp

2. U.S Department of Education, Institute of Education Sciences. (n.d.). *Schools and staffing survey (SASS). Table 4. Percentage of 2004–05 public school teacher stayers, movers, and leavers who strongly or somewhat agreed with statements about their 2003–04 base year school and 2004–05 current school.* National Center for Education Statistics. Retrieved February 25, 2009, from http://nces.ed.gov/surveys/sass/ tables/tfs_2005_04.asp

3. U.S. Department of Education, Institute of Education Sciences. (n.d.). *Digest of education statistics: 2007. Table 153. The number and percentage of students suspended from U.S. public elementary and secondary schools in 2004 by sex, race/ethnicity and state.* National Center for Education Statistics. Retrieved October 18, 2008, from http://nces.ed.gov/programs/digest/d07/tables/dt07_153.asp

4. Ibid.

5. U.S. Department of Education, Institute of Education Sciences. (n.d.). *Digest of education statistics: 2007. Table 152. The number and percentage of students expelled from public elementary and secondary schools in 2004 by sex, race/ethnicity and state: 2004.*

National Center for Education Statistics. Retrieved October 18, 2008, from http://nces.ed.gov/programs/digest/d07/tables/dt07_152.asp

6. Thompson, G. L. (2004). *Through ebony eyes: What teachers need to know but are afraid to ask about African American students.* San Francisco: Jossey Bass.

7. U.S. Department of Education, Institute of Education Sciences. *Indicators of school crime and safety: 2007. Table 12.1 Percentage of public and private school teachers who agreed or strongly agreed that student misbehavior and student tardiness and class cutting interfered with their teaching, by selected teacher and school characteristics: Various school years, 1987–88 through 2003–04.* National Center for Education Statistics. Retrieved October 18, 2008, from http://nces.ed.gov/programs/crimeindicators/crimeindicators2007/tables/table_12_1.asp?referrer=report

8. Kunjufu, J. (1990). *Countering the conspiracy to destroy black boys* (Vols. Chicago: African American Images; Kunjufu, J. (2005). *Keeping black b special education.* Chicago: African American Images.

9. Thompson, G. L. (2007). *Up where we belong: Helping African American and L students rise in school and in life.* San Francisco: Jossey Bass.

10. Delpit, L. (1995). *Other people's children: Cultural conflict in the classroom.* New York: The New Press.

11. Ferguson, A. A. (2001). *Bad boys: Public schools in the making of black masculinity.* Ann Arbor: University of Michigan Press.

12. Thompson, G. L. (2001). *African American teens discuss their schooling experiences.* Westport, CT: Bergin & Garvey.

13. Stone, J. (2007). *When she was white: The true story of a family divided by race.* New York: Miramax Books.

Chapter 7

1. Taylor, K., & Walton, S. (n.d.). Test your attitude: Eliminating our own negative feelings about standardized tests can actually help our students do better on them. *Scholastic News.* Retrieved March 2, 2009, from http://content.scholastic.com/browse/article.jsp?id=4017, p. 1.

2. Moon, T. R., Brighton, C. M., Jarvis, J. M., & Hall, C. J. State standardized testing programs: Their effects on teachers and students. Retrieved Mach 9, 2009, from University of Connecticut Neag Center for Gifted Education and Talent Development Web site: http://www.gifted.uconn.edu/nrcgt/moonbrja.html, p. 2.

3. U.S. Department of Education, Institute of Education Sciences. (n.d.). *Schools and staffing Survey (SASS). Table 4. Percentage of 2004–05 public school teacher stayers, movers, and leavers who strongly or somewhat agreed with statements about their 2003–04 base year school and 2004–05 current school.* National Center for Education Statistics. Retrieved February 25, 2009, from http://nces.ed.gov/surveys/sass/tables/tfs_2005_04.asp, p. 1.

4. Moon, T. R., Brighton, C. M., Jarvis, J. M., & Hall, C. J. (n.d.). *State standardized testing programs: Their effects on teachers and students.* Retrieved March 9, 2009, from University of Connecticut Neag Center for Gifted Education and Talent Development Web site: http://www.gifted.uconn.edu/nrcgt/moonbrja.html, p. 2.

5. Ibid., 3

6. Thompson, G. L. (2007). *Up where we belong: Helping African American and Latino students rise in school and in life.* San Francisco: Jossey Bass.

7. PBS Frontline. *Interview: Claude Steele.* Retrieved March 13, 2009, from http://www.pbs.org/wgbh/pages/frontline/shows/sats/interviews/steele.html

8. Thompson, G. L. (2007). *Up where we belong: Helping African American and Latino students rise in school and in life.* San Francisco: Jossey Bass.

9. Ibid.

10. Aronson, J. (n.d.). *Stereotype threat.* The School of Education, Center of Excellence Commitment, Leadership, Diversity. New York University. Retrieved March 10, 2009, from www.respyn.uanl.mx/especiales/2007/ee-13-2007/documentos/03.pdf, p. 1.

11. PBS Frontline. *Interview: Claude Steele.* PBS. Retrieved March 13, 2009, from http://www.pbs.org/wgbh/pages/frontline/shows/sats/interviews/steele.html, p. 3.

12. Thompson, G. L. (2007). *Up where we belong: Helping African American and Latino students rise in school and in life.* San Francisco: Jossey Bass.

13. Oakley, B. (2008). *Evil genes: Why Rome fell, Hitler rose, Enron failed, and my sister stole my mother's boyfriend.* Amherst, NY: Prometheus.

14. PBS Frontline. *Interview: Claude Steele.* Retrieved March 13, 2009, from http://www.pbs.org/wgbh/pages/frontline/shows/sats/interviews/steele.html, p. 10.

15. Aronson, J. (n.d.). *Stereotype Threat.* The School of Education, Center of Excellence Commitment, Leadership, Diversity. New York University. Retrieved March 10, 2009, from www.respyn.uanl.mx/especiales/2007/ee-13-2007/documentos/03.pdf

16. Taylor, K., & Walton, S. (n.d.). Test your attitude: Eliminating our own negative feelings about standardized tests can actually help our students do better on them. *Scholastic News.* Retrieved March 2, 2009, from http://content.scholastic.com/browse/article.jsp?id=4017, p. 1.

17. Ibid., 2.

18. Glendale Community College. (n.d). *Study skills: Strategies for test taking.* Retrieved February 28, 2009, from http://www.glendale.edu/new/services/counseling/tests.htm

19. Ibid.

20. University of Minnesota Duluth, Student Handbook. (n.d.). *Test taking strategies.* Retrieved February 28, 2009, from http://www.d.umn.edu/kmc/student/loon/acad/strat/test_take.html

21. Duke, N. K., & Ritchhart, R. (n.d.). No pain, high gain: Standardized test preparation. *Scholastic News.* Retrieved February 28, 2009, from http://www2.scholastic.com/browse/article.jsp?id=4006, pp. 2–3.

22. Scholastic. (n.d.). *Test-taking strategies for three subject areas.* Retrieved February 28, 2009, from http://www2.scholastic.com/browse/article.jsp?id=8091

23. Ibid.

24. Thompson, G. L. (2007). *Up where we belong: Helping African American and Latino students rise in school and in life* (p. 3). San Francisco: Jossey Bass.

25. Martin, J. (n.d.). Reducing test anxiety. *The Black Collegian Online.* Retrieved March 1, 2009, from http://www.black-collegian.com/study/professor_joe/projoeanxiety201.shtml, pp. 1–2.

26. Fair Test. (n.d.). *Norm-referenced achievement tests.* Cambridge, MA: Fair Test: The National Center for Fair & Open Testing. Retrieved January 15, 2005, from http://www.fairtest.org/norm-referenced-achievement-tests

27. Popham, W. J. (2004, November). A game without winners. *Educational Leadership, 62*(3), pp. 46–50.

28. Ibid.

29. PBS Frontline. *Interview: Claude Steele.* Retrieved March 13, 2009, from http://www.pbs.org/wgbh/pages/frontline/shows/sats/interviews/steele.html, pp. 15–16.

30. Ibid., 17.

31. North Central Regional Educational Laboratory. *Teacher Effectiveness.* Retrieved March 9, 2009, from http://www.ncrel.org/sdrs/areas/issues/content/cntareas/reading/li71k15.htm. Retrieved March 9, 2009, pp. 1–2.

Chapter 8

1. Kunjufu, J. (1990). *Countering the conspiracy to destroy black boys* (Vols. 1–3). Chicago: African American Images; Kunjufu, J. (2005). *Keeping black boys out of special education.* Chicago: African American Images.

2. Ferguson, A. A. (2001). *Bad boys: Public schools in the making of black masculinity.* Ann Arbor: University of Michigan Press.

3. Hale, J. E. (2001). *Learning while black: Creating educational excellence for African American children.* Baltimore: Johns Hopkins University Press.

4. Noguera, P. (2002). The trouble with black boys: The role and influence of environmental and cultural factors on the academic performance of African American males. *In Motion Magazine.* Retrieved December 8, 2006, from http://www.inmotionmagazine.com/er/pntroub1.html

5. Kunjufu, J. (1990). *Countering the conspiracy to destroy black boys* (Vols. 1–3). Chicago: African American Images.

6. Thompson, G. L. (2007). *Up where we belong: Helping African American and Latino students rise in school and in life* (p. 191). San Francisco: Jossey Bass.

Index

CORWIN

A SAGE Company

The Corwin logo—a raven striding across an open book—represents the union of courage and learning. Corwin is committed to improving education for all learners by publishing books and other professional development resources for those serving the field of PreK–12 education. By providing practical, hands-on materials, Corwin continues to carry out the promise of its motto: **"Helping Educators Do Their Work Better."**